About the author

Tiffany Beese has been a self-employed clinician (naturopath, Ortho-Bionomist) for over twenty years in New Zealand. Originally from London, she travelled the world, staying in many places. She lived in an Ashram for six months learning and teaching yoga, learning to meditate, and then continuing on the practice. This made her ready for training in the Akashic Records. Once more comfortable, she was instructed by the Ascended Masters to sit at the computer and allow the words to flow. So came knowledge and answers of commonly asked questions. Enjoy.

SEEING, FEELING, HEARING AND BEING WITH SPIRIT

Tiffany Beese

SEEING, FEELING, HEARING AND BEING WITH SPIRIT

Vanguard Press

VANGUARD PAPERBACK

© Copyright 2020
Tiffany Beese

The right of Tiffany Beese to be identified as author of
this work has been asserted by her in accordance with the
Copyright, Designs and Patents Act 1988.

All Rights Reserved

No reproduction, copy or transmission of this publication
may be made without written permission.
No paragraph of this publication may be reproduced,
copied or transmitted save with the written permission of the publisher, or in
accordance with the provisions
of the Copyright Act 1956 (as amended).

Any person who commits any unauthorised act in relation to
this publication may be liable to criminal
prosecution and civil claims for damages.

A CIP catalogue record for this title is
available from the British Library.

ISBN 978 1 784658 17 5

*Vanguard Press is an imprint of
Pegasus Elliot MacKenzie Publishers Ltd.*
www.pegasuspublishers.com

First Published in 2020

**Vanguard Press
Sheraton House Castle Park
Cambridge England**

Printed & Bound in Great Britain

Contents

Introduction 9
1 And so it Began by Arnoah 11
2 Part 2 And so it Began by Arnoah 15
3. Stones by Merlin (Ascended Master) 18
4 Psychometry by Merlin 22
5. Vibrations by Arnoah 26
6. Colour by Merlin 31
7. Guides by Quan Yin (Ascended Master) 37
8. Feelings by Quan Yin 41
9. The Bigger Picture by Arnoah 46
10. Trust and Love by Archangel Raphael 49
11. Challenges and Questions by Arnoah 54
12. Guides and Loved ones, Past Lives by Quan Yin 58
13. Compassion by Arnoah 63
14. Growth by Melchizedek 68
15. Lives by Arnoah 71
16. Love and Differences by Mother Mary 79
17. Relationships by Quan Yin 83
18. The Arts 91 by Arnoah 91
19. Religion by Arnoah 95
20. Truth by Archangel Micheal 101
21. Sentiment and Affront by Arnoah 105
22. Disease and Contracts by Quan Yin 110
23. Learning and Practice by Quan Yin and Archangel Micheal
.... 115

24. Tarot by Oshun 120
25. Death by Arnoah 124
26. Others by Arnoah 129
27. Solace and Symbols by Isis and Arnoah 133
28. Hello and Explanations by Arnoah 139
29. Advice by Arnoah 143
30. Conclusion by Arnoah and Quan Yin 147
31. The Last Word by Arnoah 149
32. Leberia by Arnoah 152
33. Feelings by Quan Yin (extra) 154

Introduction

We are what humans call God, and there is a heaven that we call Source. They are two of the same thing. We are all part of Source as you are. Your souls are made by energy coming together to become individual orbs of light. Then as humans form new offspring the soul light enters into these new ones.

As humans your different religious sects; Christianity, Catholicism, Islam, Judaism and Hinduism have all written a book in the name of their God. In actual fact we are that, God to you all. Coming together as a collective at Source (Heaven) Mohammed, Jesus, Mother Mary, Zeus and Krishna. We are all one, you are a part of this, us, energy soul connection.

All human and animal life has a connection with Source, with God. We are one of the same. We appear differently to different people in the way that they understand and will not be scared.

Understand that these Ascended Masters are able to give messages in the Akashic Records where many have been able to access. We come to you to channel these words from an observing standpoint. Anything we say is not judgmental, but comes from love and observations of your actions and reactions.

In this publication we communicate with you through her — Tiffany Beese. This has been done many times throughout history. (*How to read the Akashic Records,* Linda Howe. (2010. Sound True Inc).
This is not a new concept the way this book has been channeled and recorded. These are words of how to help people and understand the world.

There is no scientific proof of who and what we are. However, mediums, clairvoyants and channelers all confer with us. We exist in other dimensions. This is how it is.

My name is Arnoah, and I am of a race many thousands of light years away. The Akashic Records are where we can come to communicate with humans.

This book is to empower and enable yourselves to be your authentic self. Through these tools learn your purpose, activate hidden gifts (tarot, psychrometry, seeing auras, reading semi-precious stones or crystals as well as energetic healing using symbols) and help others with compassion, acceptance and love.

Enjoy…

1

And so it Began
by Arnoah

And so it began... In the beginning when time began there was always, and there still is, a greater power in the other universes that watch over many other planets. We come from love and acceptance of all. We (the Ascended Masters, Guides, passed Loved ones and interplanetary souls — Arnoah) gave you choice and the decisions you make are all your own. We want you to feel what your heart and soul is telling you, in order to get rid of all the trappings and hindrances around you. Be who you truly are. Work through your contracts in order to be pure and free of any lessons that you need to learn in this lifetime. A clearing must happen in order to get to the pure essence of yourself. Peel back the layers and feel your gift.

There are many gifts that have come to many of you. The light workers are on this earth to help and assist the others learning to give support and lessons in order to assist with your ascendance.

We come from pure love and divine intention. We are here to assist you in your development of your gift for the greater good.

Only to be used for good, these gifts that we speak of, come from a place of integrity.

Do not let your EGO take hold. We are here to support you in your learning and to aid the development of your skills. Ask and you shall find the answers by sitting quietly, and being able to hear what we are saying. Notice coincidences, notice comparisons, see and feel the contrast of what is around you. Relax in the space, feel the different vibrations of all that is around you.

Sit quietly and be...

Hold your space — it takes perseverance to be consistent in the practice. Set a month aside where you can minimise the amount of toxins that are in your body.

Follow what your body wants; ask yourself a question before you consume something. Do you really want it? Do you really need it?

Drink more water, eat less meat. The vibration of the meat changes the inner soul. On a vibrational level the animal has probably been killed in fear, the cortisol (stress hormone) has been travelling around its body when it was killed. The waiting animals can smell their fellow's fear. If you must eat meat to survive even for that month make sure it is happy meat (free-range, or home-killed.) However, for a short period of time we are sure you will be able to survive (30 days).

Sit in a comfortable position, spine straight, in a chair, on the floor, legs crossed, with a cushion under your seat and against something firm or even on your back with the spine straight. This enables the free flow of energy from the divine, higher self to come through and circulate through the body. Wait... Wait... Wait... we will come.

Surround yourself with white light from your toes, from the Gaia (mother earth), to the top of your head and above. Eighteen inches above (the 8th chakra) the bridge to the other world that you can feel but not see.

Breathe.

Allow the monkey chatter to come, but do not engage in a conversation with it. Instead notice and bring yourself back to the breath or your focus.

If you are having problems starting or continuing, use Solfeggio frequencies.

(Solfeggio 9 tones emotional and physical healing.)
- Connecting the dots and realisation of situations (174 Hz),
- Expressing Uniqueness (285 Hz)
- Infinite Wisdom (396 Hz)
- Wipes out negative energy, love is infinite potential (432 Hz)
- Universal Healing, manifest your greatness (528 Hz)
- Shine your light (639 Hz)
- Removes toxins, the all-seeing you (741 Hz)
- Let go of fear, over thinking and worries/cleansing (852 Hz)

- Universal Oneness (963 Hz)

Ask and we will come; ask for help; ask for concentration; it takes practice.

We know that these things don't come easily especially with all the input with social media, and the brain dances from thing to thing. The mind jumps about, the ego doesn't want to be turned off. It wants to control. Take control from your heart, (your master,) and from your soul (your teacher).

Try to focus on the heart or the soul, whichever feels the most comfortable; whichever resonates with you the best. What do you notice? Take a pen and paper to write things down that you see, feel, and hear. Go in with no questions, no hidden agenda, no prerequisite outcome. There will be days where nothing happens, where you thought it was futile and a waste of time. IT ISN'T. Every meditation or concentration session is never a waste of time. On some level there will be a change.

It's the ego that is struggling with suppression caused by what you are doing. It's the ego that lives in volatile emotion, it's the ego that is telling you false truths. The student, and that is what the ego is… is trying to take over, it doesn't want to be smothered. (Reminds us of a teenager who has been in a job for six months and believes they know everything). Ego wants a voice to keep you in the shallow space that it has become accustomed to. It likes mean, shallow, selfish thoughts. It likes hedonism. In order for the heart and soul to come forward the ego has to take a step back. Remember, just like a narcissist it will come back stronger and stronger every time you try to suppress it. It can be so loud that nothing else can be heard. So the soul and heart wait patiently because they aren't going anywhere. They are with you for life, but the ego comes and goes. Think of it like a small child that doesn't get its way. You can either relinquish your power, and let it take over-eating all the sugary things, the alcohol, the shit food that gives an instantaneous hit — or you can take the word and desire of the teacher and master and provide them with the right nutrition. You will know your own right combination. Listen carefully to your inner, true self — your authentic self and raise your vibration above the ego and bypass it to the really good emotions and feeelings of laughter and joyful experiences. The amazing memories from meaningful experiences. The noticing of nature around you with gratitude. The relationships that has true meaning, true validation. The stuff that gives you clarity and strength. The knowing (inner wisdom) that you are okay and of value that makes you more resilient to be able to stand in your own true power in order to bring light and love to those that are around you.

You will feel freer than you ever have before. Stronger, no matter what is thrown at you. You will be able to recognise others that come from a place of ego; that want only small instant gains and to sometimes be deliberately hurtful. Feel your inner self, and trust that the outcome, no matter what it is, has happened for a reason. Even though it may not be what you think it should be, wait and trust that the correct outcome, down the line, will be right for you.

DO NOT TRUST EGO. It is the child, the student and we don't want an inexperienced political candidate running your world, but instead an energy that has been around for a while, which knows the pros and cons of running a country politically, economically and environmentally and can see the long picture; not the here and now rewards.

As with everything, it takes practice. Practice to turn the ego off; practice to hearing your heart and soul's messages; practice to turn off the monkey chatter.

Trust it will come.

2

Part 2
And so it Began by Arnoah

When we, the Ascended Masters, come down to see what earth is doing we are upset. What has been changed and created is not from a place of integrity. We are here to help and show you how to make a difference. Go about your own life with integrity and truth. Show how it is done around others so that they may learn from you and see how you behave in certain circumstances; how you choose the right way, not the way of the ego.

Allow your friends to talk and be around you, notice their vibration. How high does it resonate? Do you feel comfortable sitting with them? Is there anything they can teach you? We allow and your contract allows meetings; be they small, momentary or long term, developing a friendship over many years. All meetings have a purpose. It is up to you to fathom out why it has happened. The meeting could be good or bad, it is just an experience to learn from, to remember how it felt, how the vibration was with you when you met. As a light worker or an apprentice light worker it is up to you to notice and be a part of what is happening. What do you need to learn from this meeting? It may not be apparent right then and there, but information that they have given you — good or bad — will be useful later. You may not know it yet. Do not dismiss nonchalantly, there is a reason that this meeting had to happen.

Understanding your true self is what it is about. Accepting what is good and bad in you, that what makes you perfect in the here and now. ACCEPTANCE of all equals, have no judgement, as you understand what God is, or Source. We do not judge. This is a man-made concept and it is for ruling the masses. Everybody goes to heaven or Source, where the souls hang out, where they figure out their contract and what they need to learn now or in the next lifetime. These lives are to build on and on over many lifetimes. As there are many different experiences then there are many lives. In one lifetime you cannot possibly complete all experiences, all emotions, all good and bad occurrences. There are now light-workers that are on their last life and this we are thankful for as the population is growing and more and more people need their guidance. No one needs judgement on how to feel and get through their lifetime. We watch from all around, we try to teach those who will listen. Those who want to learn to grow, to be selfish or self preserving but at the same time stand in their power. We want you to grow and support Gaia, to quietly go through life gently influencing what you can for the better. To not support hedonistic decisions, to not aid and support what young souls think they want to do. Follow the master, follow the teacher, they are linked into the Source or Heaven as some religions call it, and again, listen quietly and you will hear. ACCEPTANCE is the hardest lesson but the lesson that is learnt and never denied again. Once you find true acceptance it is really hard to become judgemental again. Allowing space and time for others to do their thing. If you don't agree then there in itself may be a judgement… Look at yourself before you look at others. If you find you are coming from a place of integrity and no personal gain then you are standing in the right place and vibration. However, if your relationship changes with the other,(perhaps you take a step back and have ill thoughts about that person, or you just don't like them anymore) then there is a judgement. Even God does not judge, although time and time again man has said that we do. WHY? WHY? WHY?

Notice yourself in the feelings and replies — does it seem judgemental? kind but not a pushover. This is standing in your power. (This means know yourself, limitations and influences so that you are true to yourself, your ideals and that you do not get persuaded to do something that you are not comfortable with.) If they call you selfish then they have made a judgement on you. Give unconditionally if you do give. Trust your teacher and master not the student. Quietly go forth in this world and gently change the vibration so that others can feel comforted by your presence and your voice soothes in times of trouble. Trust your heart and soul and the words will flow. Don't think — allow the words to flow. You may not feel present when this is happening but trust that the words are coming from us, from Source.

We want to assist you in the preservation of Gaia, we want you to see all your grandchildren in a healthy environment. Clean air, clean earth, clean water. We see it can be done but slowly and steadily it will come to pass.

Write to newspapers and on social media and point out how things can be helped and assisted. If more people raise their vibration then more will join and see how it is to live in this way. Calmly, patiently, consistently (with practice it will become second nature). Remember, acceptance is the key. Even though the Earth is in the shit at the moment you can save it, quietly, gently and efficiently. Once the powers that are there currently move on then the new generation will form new governments and new conservational laws to protect. The energies at the moment will see more and more people die — those who do not listen, those who are pure hedonists, those who don't give a shit will find troubling times ahead of them. Accept this for them and allow them to see the truth in their way or they will reincarnate again.

Be who you truly are. Compromise if the end game is worth it. Accept those who you don't see eye to eye with you, but help and assist them to knowledge. Remember your knowledge may be different to theirs but know that the end game is in both your sights. It's just a different path. As long as there is integrity, honesty and truth then all will work out in the end.

World powers will start to crumble as the new generation comes through — trust that we have a game plan and that we will be with you all the way. We will not desert you when times are tough, but instead call on us and we will help with your resilience and truth. The Light will conquer all.

And so it is…

3.

Stones by Merlin (Ascended Master)

These semi-precious crystals and certain stones (amethyst, opal, garnet) are amazing sources of energy. Individual stones aid and assist individual people. Do not under estimate the resonance and power of these semi-precious stones. They can help people in a subtle and complete way. Allow their energy to infiltrate all that is of the persons' body. They need to relax and give it a go. Sit in the pyramidal shape or lie flat, place the crystal on a part of your body that hurts or have it in your hands that are relaxed and without tension. One may not feel the benefits straight away but they will gradually change the vibration. There will be subtle signs, aches will start to diminish and the mind will start processing the vibration. The higher self will feel supported.

 Find a stone that you feel akin to. Go to a store or market place to find the right one. Or it may be a few. You will know and listen to the master and teacher NOT the student. Cleanse the stone in different ways, moon, water, sun, rain and anything that is natural and it will cleanse what it needs to. It is about trust and belief. Actually, you don't have to believe, you just have to be. Listed below are essential stones that will be beneficial to you. We want you to be quiet and feel the stones. Notice if there is any vibration still on the stone. If it doesn't feel right, then cleanse again. Trust your higher self, do not second guess but trust.

 Hold the stone in your right hand at first and feel what is going on. Find contrast with different stones notice the subtle vibration of each stone.

 If you don't feel a difference then put the stone down, drink some water and go into a meditation. Hold the stone in your hand or if lying down place it on your solar plexus and notice anything going on. We will guide you and direct you to feel the stones. Ask and you shall receive the knowledge at the appropriate time for you. There is no right or wrong there only is…

Amethyst is a really good one to start with however if it truly doesn't resonate with you pick another.

Rose quartz is also very powerful and relatively cheap for beginning your practice. Once you become accustomed to the feel then you can go on to read others' stones. This becomes Psychometry. Trust and you shall feel. Empty your mind and allow the pictures or words to come through. Don't think — feel. Allow the space, the nothingness to be filled with the knowledge that we are trying to convey to you.

Stones	Energetic Action	Energetic Physical
Amethyst vibration of 3	Spirituality and contentment, facilitates transmutation of lower to higher frequencies.	Balances intellectual, emotional and physical bodies. Bestows stability, strength, invigoration and peace.
Calcite vibration of 8	Electrical amplifier, helps the mind and body remember astral travel and channelling.	Ameliorates disease of the kidneys, pancreas and spleen. Clears chakras, amplifies energies.
Garnet vibration of 2	Stone of health, extracts negative energy from chakras, and transmutes energy to a beneficial state.	Balances and stimulates the Kundalini, and the crown to ensure free flow. Discourages disruptive, chaotic and disorganised growth.
Hematite vibration of 9	Mental atunement, memory enhancement, original thinking and technical knowledge.	Balances yin-yang energies, focuses and provides stability between ethereal and physical nervous systems.

Lapis Lazuli vibration of 3	Activation & energising of the throat and brow chakras. Creativity and expansion of the perfectness of self.	Stimulates emotional, mental and physical purity and clarity. Supports the advancement of universal wisdom.
Muscovite vibration of 1	Stimulates the heart chakra, allowing layers of insecurities to disperse. Lessens self-doubt.	Quick thinking, succinct & precise expression. Strengthens the intuitive process.
Obsidian-snowflake vibration of 8	Breaks unnecessary patterns. Brings balance and purity to body, mind and spirit.	Aids with serenity and isolation to surrender to a meditative state: love & beauty.
Oynx vibration of 7	Aligns the total person with higher powers. Banish grief, enhance self-control, aids wise decision making.	Encourages happiness and good fortune. Promotes recognition of personal strengths, aids with becoming master of your own future.
Pyrite vibration of 9	A defence stone, which shields from negative energy — on the physical, etheric, and emotional level.	Assists one to see beyond the facades, lies of words or actions. Truth seeker.
Quartz —rose, smokey, Vibration 7, 2/8	Smokey promotes good business, and psychic abilities, atunement of 3rd eye activity and removes obstacles.	Rose offers love, compassion, kindness and tenderness. Nurturing & self-love.
Selenite vibration of 8	Expands one's self-awareness, clarity of the mind, flexibility of one's	Provides insight & assists in issues of judgements.

Selenite contd.	nature and strength to decisions.	Reconnection between the conscious self & mystic self — super consciousness.
Turquoise vibration of 1	Strengthens and aligns all chakras, meridians and subtle bodies. Brings any & all energies to a higher level. Induces wisdom and understanding.	Healer of the spirit, soothing the energy and bringing peace of mind. Balances male/female energies. Increases psychic powers.

This information is readily available, the vibration refers to the numerology of the spelling of the crystal. Some information from *"Love is in Earth" — Melody (1995)* — Earth-Love Publishing House

We, the Ascended Masters, vibrate the stones for you so that you may read them for people, to help with guidance or acceptance of themselves. Please do feel the crystals or stones for yourselves often as practice. The stones allow the imprint of yourself onto them. And the imprint of others as they hold them, read and feel how they are in the stone. Keep them in your pocket for at least a day or on your body to pick up the vibration of yourself. Do this once you have cleansed them after buying from a crystal store. It is important to neutralise any vibrations first before you start to read them. To read sit in a quiet place with that person. Take their crystal into your left hand then hold between the two hands. Find the nothingness in the mind. Breathe. Allow what you feel in your body come through. Any emotions you may feel speak of them. If you see a video in your mind's eye — describe it. Words may come and so just speak them. It may only be a couple or a few words but allow them to come out. Remember to have no attachment to what you are saying. What will make no sense to you may mean a lot to them. Take your time and allow things to arise in the nothingness of your mind. Practice.

Trust your inner guidance, trust us. We are with you every step of the way.

And so it is…

4

Psychometry
by Merlin

We know there are troubling times ahead but what we are about to say will help you with resilience and inner strength to carry on the work that your contract has specified. We want you to know that we are here for you, all you have to do is ask. Learning more of these skills will give you confidence and more resilience against what may lie ahead.

We want you to understand Psychometry and how it works. Everything from this earth has the capacity to take on energy from the person who is wearing it or carrying it around with them. It can be found in any form, jewellery, meaningful possesions and things that you have an emotional attachment to. The vibration of that object will take on your vibration and an act as a conductor of your energy and feelings both past and future. Be quiet and still and hold the object in your right hand or cup it between both hands. Sit, wait and feel what is happening. You may see visions or pictures or you may get words. Emotions and feelings are easier to pick up. They are all vibrations; different resonances of your emotions. Each feeling or emotion has a different frequency and it is up to you to read that frequency and interpret those waves.

Try and feel the emotion and what it brings up for you. Be aware about how your emotion reacts in your body. Different people will have different interpretations. Take down notes at first when learning; but you will find it becomes more comfortable with each reading. Practice with your friends, colleagues, and acquaintances. Building up your confidence with the people you do know, allowing what you feel and becoming more comfortable in translating what there is for people. Once you have more confidence you can then work with others that you do not know and trusting what is revealed. The reading starts with a clean slate and less bias. You will have no preconceived ideas about what you think you may discover.

Be careful with this. With each practice or reading you will become more finely tuned. Notice and compare with each experience you have. Remember if the visions come from your own personal experience, and your own selective perception then it is not theirs it it yours Be careful, don't bring that in. Go to the nothingness and allow visuals, words or feelings to come through. Your understanding of a situation could be subjective as drawing off your own experiences and not related to their life experiences. They will have different dynamics and what is meaningful to them may not be to you.

Be aware of your own ego or trying to impress the person you are reading for. If you can't see or feel anything then say so. Do not feel you have to come up with something. Go in with no expectations, allow things to flow and just express what you see, hear or feel. Remember if what you experience doesn't make sense to you it may make sense to the person you are reading. Again, there is no right or wrong; there only is.

Allow yourself time and quiet at first and allow things to flow. If you are trying too hard it will become forced and not real. Feel with tenderness, what is being given to you. Trust that it is coming through you. See what is filling in the hole of nothingness in your mind, allow the nothingness to be gradually filled with information that you need to express. Almost become one with that object so that your vibrations meld together to really feel and understand what information is being provided. Be cautious about what is given if it is unpleasant and let it sit with them in a gentle way. We do not want to turn these people away to speak badly of us as we are only trying to help and give them warnings and understanding of themselves.

If you can sit crossed legged in a pyramid shape your seat on a cushion and your back against something firm with your spine straight — this is the most powerful, as this grounds you and keeps the energy within you. Hold the object close in your hands and be. Be careful of your interpretation but remember that practice is the key. Just like any activity, it all takes practice, practice, practice.

Feel the shape of the object, the texture and the temperature. What information is it relaying to you?

Use your fingerpads as collectors of information, (There is more sensitivity than the tips, more surface area and sensation receptors) as you practice the fingers will become accustomed to reading objects through touch and the sensory cortex. Gradually your brain will learn more, pick up more and relay more.

Keys are hard if it is a bunch however a single house key to the person's house may tell you more than the person may want to hear. You need to define what they want to know. You may pick up the houses' vibration rather than the owner of the house. This you will have to discern for yourself with experience and practice.

Please remember this is not an ego exercise; it is the higher self, trying to communicate with you the information the person has asked you about. If there is some information that you feel is quite negative then be sensitive when you relay this back especially if you think this person will respond badly. It is better to say nothing if that person is evil or bad and walk away. You will know when this needs to happen; again, follow your master or teacher. It is not your job to change or judge that person, it is your job to just be with them without prejudice and judgement. Only truly egotistical people judge and put down others. This is a lesson they will have to learn elsewhere.

You can also practice with things in nature itself. Try the vibration of a tree, a river or the countryside. Sit and feel with your whole body what nature is telling you. You speak of tree huggers, we like that term, it brings you closer to nature, helps you feel Gaia, links you in with the surroundings and the beauty that is everywhere. ACCEPT what you see and feel. It is a really good place to start. It is also good that your feet are on the earth to ground yourself when you first begin. We welcome you to practice and share with nature. Then you can go on to people and things. All things made of this earth have vibration. Plastic is difficult as a man-made material is harder to read, but any elements from the periodic table will have vibrations as these were made when this world was formed in perfection. It is still perfection as Gaia goes through this transformation at the moment but with help from light workers and others you can make it a better place.

Help us to raise the vibration of Gaia, help us raise the vibration of those around you to be able to live together and with no prejudice or judgement. However, remember that at the moment, it is perfect, as you are in every moment, it is how it should be right now, right here. Especially if following the soul (teacher).

Using the Psychometry skill will also bring more awareness to more people in the world perhaps showing them that there are other things that science cannot prove and will open their minds to other possibilities. There are many possibilities you have not seen, and neither will you see nor experience them all; that is another contract.

Teach your children this skill from early on as they are not influenced so much by social restraints and social norms. Adults often pooh, pooh a child's imaginary friend. They are often not imaginary, they are spirits or passed loved ones that have come to help the child in their need, whatever that may be at the time. (*The author has been in contact with several people and they saw "a special" friend. I (the author/channeler have seen in my practice room child clients that have brought them with them. When asked the child to describe their friend it was a confirmation of what I was seeing.)*

This is another way of opening the new generation to our lessons and teachings. Listen to them, do not negate them. Encourage them to tell you about it, encourage them to speak without fear but also listen to them without judgement or prejudice.

All children are the future, the future to protect Gaia, the future to make a better place, the future to help save Gaia. The future holds so many great possibilities, allow space and time to let things evolve. Be patient, and allow space for this.

And so it is…

5.

Vibrations
by Arnoah

What we want to talk to you about today is equality... We do not understand how people can be judgemental and cruel to others, how they can mistreat those who they feel are lesser than themselves, when in actual fact they are not. They are just on a different contract from you. Different experiences are to be had by different people in order for them to learn and become a greater, kinder, less judgemental and more accepting person. These lessons are sometimes hard to accept. Again, ego has reared its ugly head. However, we should like you to have a little ego so that you can get up each day and be proud of who you are and happy about what you have accomplished so far in this life. With a little ego that keeps testing you, therefore enabling you to recognise when it steps in, noticing where the thoughts come from, then adjust accordingly to continue to grow your communication with your heart and soul.

Unfortunately, people don't like to speak their truth because of feelings that may hurt others. But if you stand in your own power speaking the truth, we hope that they will learn from that lesson and consider what the other is talking about. We see you standing in your power and a white light comes around you to protect and guide. Allow yourself to channel those words of truth as you feel it and for the greater good. Sometimes as light workers you need to point out simple elements that they may be missing of themselves or are afraid of feeling as it may hurt too much. Yes, it does hurt as the other person will have to relinquish the old patterns, recognising traits of the ego and allow those hurts be heard then let go with acceptance, learn from them so as not to repeat and come into the new order, the new vibrations of their internal being. Be who they truly are. Try not to falter from the path and feel what is being channelled into you about the situation or for that person. Trust that we know and will help you stand tall and proud. Behind your belief system is something that is so huge, so great that the human brain cannot always totally comprehend. But the greatness, the love and the truth are all behind you. We are here to stand behind you when the truth is hard. You will feel it in your gut. At the very core of you. Do not deny this part. This is very important for their growth. However, choose your words carefully and be the vehicle of the truth from us.

These skills of truth speaking are part of becoming a light worker: our disciples and we are one. There is a hierarchy of knowledge, wisdom and growth for every individual. We are all one but we are different levels of that one. However, we treat everyone the same but show knowledge to those who are ready. As humans learn different things at different levels. Some need simple guidance and others are further along their journey and are ready to hear or have more complicated lessons, or explanations. Trust our guidance system, trust what you know.

You will feel sick and unhappy if you do not follow your calling; the soul will shrivel over time and you will get sick. If you do not allow love in, then you will not grow. There are many different forms of love. You will know when you feel this. There is love for your children, love for humankind, love for your spouse, and love for your family. All are different in interpretation but all come from Source. We are love. There is no hate nor fear here at Source. F.E.A.R (False Evidence Appears Real) leads to anger which leads to violence. This is unnecessary and what you have heard time and time again 'love conquers all' — yes eventually, but some take more time to truly feel and understand what love is than others.

We want to talk of tones, universal tones, different frequencies, and different uses of these different vibrations.

Everything has a tone or vibration, we spoke of this before. You need to practice picking up vibration from nature, from others, being able to feel that vibration is a good start. A way of feeling it first is to notice other tones and vibrations by allowing the exposure of different tones to caress your body and cells. You are predominantly made up of water, and water carries vibrations of sounds and feelings. Masaru Emoto's work was a great illustration of what you can feel and find inside water molecules. (*The Message from Water: the message from water is telling us to take a look at ourselves* — Hado 2000 ISBN9784939098000)

Lie in water, feel the ebb and flow of the pool, sea, lake or stream. Each has a different feel. Cleansing also takes place in water; clean, fresh water. What do you notice whilst there? If you notice nothing then that is okay too. Remember there is no right or wrong, there only is.

It takes practice to feel the water and the vibration just like feeling nature in the bush or countryside. Hone your skills and feel so that you can pick up on what is important. Remember, things are never what they seem at first. Look deeper, look closer.

We find 432Hz, 448Hz and 528Hz (mentioned chapter 1) very powerful along with Gamma, Alpha, Beta, Delta, and Theta soundwaves. (You Tube). These tones affect the molecules of the DNA. These tones of sound all affect the brain in some way, relaxing (Alpha 7- 13 Hz), helps focus (Beta 15 — 20Hz), aids sleep (Delta, 0.5 — 2 Hz), assists in meditation (Theta 4 — 8 Hz) and promote creativeness (Gamma 40Hz). There has been cases of Gamma 40 Hz affect Alzheimer's patients in a positive way. Sit in these tones and notice any change within. Each chakra has a tone. Sit in these tones and feel. These will help you become balanced and complete. You do this by sitting comfortably or lying, allow the tones, notes of the music to flow over you and into the body. Allow it to affect every cell. What do you feel in different parts of your body? Vibration, tingles or perhaps wooshes of air at different areas. Each chakra has a tone. These tones will help you stay calm and clear when later dealing with the outside world, that can become jarring and an assault to the system. What humans have done is wreck the world with the pollution but this had to happen for growth and completion within the human race.

We can see the end game, be it hundreds and thousands of your years ahead. Our light years are different from yours in that we orbit in a different way at this end of the universe. Time and space is a continuum for us and there are no real seasons, as you understand it. We are a constant, the universe is a constant and most remains the same in our world. Time does not exist to us, a manmade concept to keep the world in order. We understand why you had to do this to help move through space with efficiency and order. Too much chaos makes people unhappy, as you like order, you like systems, you like boundaries. Many in this world with mental issues cannot cope without structure, and this life they lead helps them to work through and to move on to the next one. For others whom have previously sampled disability in another life or even in this will perhaps to be kinder and help without prejudice of others as they experience a life with disabilities – mentally or physically.

Tone here will also help these people. The sounds will help on a level that will keep them calm and get them through this world at this time. More mental institutions and hospitals should pipe through these tones, which may help better than suppressing drugs for them. We see calm in these institutions if this is done. The tones or frequencies of 432Hz and 528Hz (Universal healing tone, if sick these will always help). And perhaps healing on a DNA and cellular level could be considered. Unfortunately, some drugs anti-depressants and anti-psychotics, which in their nature suppresses, will hinder these tones getting though on a greater level but on a micro level there will be some change somewhere.

Find the tone that resonates most with you. There are many different tones and your favourite now may become different in a couple of months. As you change through growth and understanding, peeling back the layers of lessons so your body will change its own vibration thus the tones that you listen to will change with it. Trust your inner being, your inner soul, your master and teacher. Do not trust your student — head ego. This will put smoke screens up so that you don't first recognise what is right for you.

We want you to sit in the pyramid shape, crossed legs with a cushion under your seat if that helps, prop yourself up and support your back and listen.

Allow the tone to resonate throughout your bones, feel the vibration. When listening, each of your chakra centres will be affected; feel the music. There will be more tones, with underlying music that you find easy to listen to, not so much the haunting sounds of what some think are angels, but more modern. We are adapting and changing the way the music will come to you. There is no right or wrong there is just different music over different tones.

There may be rainbow colours coming through in your mind's eye, allow these to come, notice what you see, drift off into that blissful, nirvana moment. This is when the master and teacher sing with it. We have different frequencies in our bodies at different times. No tone is constantly with you. As you change and develop so the tones change. After all you do not want to be stagnant. We see the development of your DNA with the tones, as you continue to hear, listen and feel, so the DNA will begin to change for your skills as a light worker; gradually you will change and develop. We are excited that because of these words more people will try it and more will become caretakers of Gaia. We are smiling, we believe it is a privilege that you have asked and are seeking more to help with this world. A place of love — mostly a place where peace can eventually be. A place where there is no judgement and prejudice. Listen and we will come closer to you. We will communicate with you and guide you to make the right decisions for you. Be still in the tones and this will really resonate with some of you at that time. It is easy and uncomplicated, no convoluted ways and rituals, the simplest is the best. Tones are the simplest way to raise your vibrations. These tones will be available to all and we want this. Spreading the word in a gentle way, in a non-verbal way. Some things don't have to be explained and tones bypass speech.

We hope you enjoy this way as music also instigates happiness but also may remind some of sadness. If this is the case then sit and allow the tears to flow and clear the baggage. We love you all.

Thank you.

6.

Colour
by Merlin

And so it is…

Today we want to talk to you of colour. There are so many different colours that can invoke all sorts of healing properties. The chakras are part of this theme and these can help or hinder the progress of yourselves. Relaying the chakra colours needs to be spoken with caution and integrity. Seeing the hues around people can be a really tale-telling tool. In the auric field you can pick up many things.

You may not see colour, but you may have a sense of colour, or feel the vibration of the energy around a person. Whilst going about your day see if you can detect any aura around colleagues or friends. This does not cross the ethical line as you are only exploring and at the moment you are not using these details for anything except observation.

Take a moment of stillness as you sit on the sidewalk and look, but you need to unfocus the eye to be able to truly see what is being revealed to you and your second sight. It is easier at first if the person is not moving, do this in meetings or church or another place where people don't really move. Check out around them first. What do you see? It is easier sometimes if they are standing in front of a plain wall with no pattern. Stare but don't stare at them, unfocus around the outside of their body. Sometimes you might see flares of colour not their perfect even shape. Different colours and shapes mean different things.

The thickness also matters, the condition of the aura, dense, thin, spacey, and holey, complete… This shows the aura around and above this person showing different colours at different places.

(given permission by Kirsty Bruce & Beyond the Veil)

(given permission by Kirsty Bruce & Beyond the Veil)

This shows where the different chakras are and which colour correlates to each centre.

Start at the top of the head or the upper torso of the person. What do you see?

Or you can focus on the third eye and see what appears around them. If focused on that one part then unfocus around the head, it will be easier to differentiate. You may at first believe that you are making it up. We believe that if you come from a place of integrity and realise that there is no point in lying, then you will be fine. REMEMBER THERE IS NO RIGHT OR WRONG you are just honing your skills.

We want you to practice. You can even do it with animals if you can get them to be still at first while you practice. Trees and nature all have an aura but first just sense their energy as we have said before, and then see if you can see colours. Gradually with your mind's eye or third eye you will be able to discern the patterns or colours. Not all of you will see colours, some will see patterns, some will just feel the energy and translate it into auras. It is a good way to discern the person and their energy and you will be informed about the person. This is a skill that takes a lot of practice. Notice the person that they are, however, this is not the be all and end all of assessing. Do not draw complete conclusions by what you see. Again, it comes down to your interpretation, not only from your past experiences but also your own prejudices.

We mentioned this before; be careful of your own prejudices, your own interpretation; make sure that there is no personal agenda in the conclusion of your reading. Personal interpretation can be dangerous. Find the emptiness, the space between the notes and allow the answer or information to come to you.

To be able to leave your baggage at the door and not bring it into the room is a skill in itself, and even the most self-professed mediums and clairvoyants are not able to do this. Again, this is why letting go of 90 % of your ego is the key. Have no opinion, no judgement, only acceptance of what is, not what you think or interpret it to be.

There are colours that we regularly see in aura reading;
Base — red,
Lower spine or navel — orange,
Solar plexus — yellow,

Heart — green,

Throat- sky blue,

Third eye — indigo and the Crown is violet.

There is an eighth and this is often pure white with flecks of colours. The flecks are often made up of any one of those colours mentioned. But again, there are no right or wrong colours.

The quality of the colours matter, the dullness or the shininess. With some people you can see a glow, these are the ones who are doing lots of practice and are clearing up their act… They are the ones who are practicing every day. It does make a difference if you meditate often, even just a few quiet moments just to centre yourself. Allowing the divine into your very being, whilst you are there. Remember, there will be some change even if you don't feel satisfied with the attempt at meditation. As we've said before it will come. Get rid of hate, arrogance, complacency. Be who your soul truly is.

The auras may be different colours at different parts of the body; they may be thinner in one area and thicker in another. You can often tell if there is an injury or a pain in the body as it can show itself in the aura. With really sick people the aura often struggles to be whole. Drugs make a difference, including pharmaceuticals and recreational. Anti-depressants and other mind-altering drugs make a difference as well. These often suppress the true electrical system in the brain and therefore the third eye and the crown chakra. The overall aura will appear holey and, in some places, incomplete or thinned out.

We understand how these drugs are deemed necessary, if you feel happy on them then all good, but it will be worth getting a second opinion if you are not sure. We know that sometimes doctors prescribe drugs as they don't know how to help them or have the wrong diagnosis *(author has talked to several people and they have been prescribed anti-depressants even though they had not complained of being depressed, or even went to the doctor for feeling sad,* (https://www.fiercehealthcare.com/hospitals-health-systems/jhu-1-3-misdiagnoses-results-serious-injury-or-death) and there may be other alternative reasons or may even be entities stuck to some of these people.

As you hone your skills and practice it may be possible to see or sense these other creatures, entities, and troubled spirits that attach themselves to you and to others. They give false results of how people are feeling and can alter and manipulate these people's aura and demeanour. Study the chakras, study colour; these all tie in with crystals and vibrations. Some see fractal patterns but mostly people see colour or shapes, it just depends on your skill or gift. Each corresponding chakra also applies to that level in the body, they overlap at times and the colour melds like a rainbow. People can feel out of sorts if the chakras are not spinning in the correct way. They should be spinning clockwise. To be able to balance your own chakras is a worthwhile skill, and if yours are balanced then the reading of other people will come more readily. When working with others to balance theirs do a short meditation on the chakras beforehand. Go through each one connecting with the point, the spot or the centre of that energy centre. Connect your mind's eye with that part of the body and sit with it. Feel and notice what is happening. Picture in your mind's eye the colour that you want to work so referring to the chakra that you are energising. Allow happy beautiful thoughts into your imagination, visualisation and place that happy vibration on to the chakra being worked on. Now when working on others; Bring in your guides and angels asking for the Divine help of all who work with you. *"Great Divine Spirit Father Mother God, I ask that you help* (name) *to greater balance for themselves. Amen"* Hold your hands over the centres one at a time. See if you can feel any energy. Visualise energy coming through you — down through the crown, and down through your arms and to your hands to their chakra with that happy visualisation. This will re-correct or reenergise the chakra centre. Be present, focused and with intent. Hold until you can feel a change or a deep breath occurs in either of you. Time with that beautiful visualisation and restorative energy and the chakra will start spinning; then work up the body with each point, each centre. See what you notice and then do the same thing again. Have a happy thought visualisation and place it on that chakra centre. Breathe and allow the energy to come through. We will do the rest.

Complete all seven chakras, each one spins in the clockwise direction. Feel the energy going through you as you get them working again. Remember, it may not happen at first and too much trying may not work, it's about allowing a space for the chakras to get a reboot. If you have been out of sorts for a while then this may not happen straight away. Keep repeating the process and you will notice a settling in you with calm.

We suggest you find one discipline to begin with and slowly expand your repertoire. Either stones, psychrometry or aura reading and healing. Whatever feels the most comfortable to you, your body, soul and your heart.

Your body is made up of electricity and the chakras rely on this to enable the spinning of them. You also have layers around you or your aura and gradually you will be able to read them on others. It is a lovely soft start to people's gift and a gentle way of introducing alternative possibilities to others. Letting friends know that there is something that you cannot see. Although we believe humans now have a camera that can discern the colours or an aura. However, this may not give a true reading.

Once you can read auras you can then begin to help people to make them whole on an energetic level and this will resonate through to the organism to start on the road to recovery.

Allow space and time to become present and skilled; practice, practice, practice as we have stated before. It's okay if you don't have the time every day but keep practicing even when you are out or in crowds. You can always work on your skills and remember it is for the greatest good not the self-fulfilling ego skill.

And so it is…

7.

Guides
by Quan Yin
(Ascended Master)

We are enjoying speaking through this book to share important information that we have for you. However, it is always your choice as to whether you follow these teachings and guidance to take the world and yourselves to a higher vibration.

What we send down to you are guides and angels to help you in your work with others. We move quietly amongst you, to help guide and steer you in your path. We are often with people who cannot see or feel us but we are around. To help you on your path of enlightenment, although we do not like this term; we prefer knowing, or wisdom. We will help you on your path and steer you clear of the wrong path by signalling through your gut, or your heart — perhaps there is a tingling or a wrenching in your gut. Perhaps even a drawing like a magnet towards things that are better for you than other choices.

It is always up to you to choose to follow your gut or the little tell-tale signs that we are with you. We would like you to listen more. Some people do really stupid things, and for that we will not take responsibility as they do not follow the higher self or their gut, or as we would also call it the teacher (heart) and the master (soul). Listen and these areas and your higher self will get messages through these parts. We are all connected; you just have to believe. It is easier for us if you do. However, magic things happen which are unexplained in science and are often misunderstood. We would like to say there are no coincidences. All things happen for a reason. If you are still enough and in meditation, we can communicate with you and your higher self. There are lots of music published that proclaim that it will help you meet your guides. If you are however not ready to meet them, they will not come forward. If that is the case you have to trust your gut more often, then we will know you will be ready. Meditation also brings awareness to hearing your heart and gut or soul. Notice your senses and feelings when making a decision — what does it feel like, what do the sensations in your body tell you? To the seers among you we often come forward to give you messages. However, some messages are received according to different people's agendas and experiences. Listen to the words and see how they resonate with you. What do you feel? Notice the contrast of your higher self or guide coming to you or your shallow immediate ego decision. How did that work out in the long run for you? What we have seen, is people taking the easy quick route for instant gains but it is not self-sustaining. Trust us — trust your higher self.

We appear as you would want us to appear, the loved ones that have crossed over and are now working with you. They are with you in the form of how they want to be seen. How they are most comfortable in their skin, so if they died at 80, they may not appear as you last saw them but actually as a younger version of themselves. We elders, come as we are. As many of the pictures that have been channelled are as we are. We are pure energy, vibration at a very high speed, so that these molecules can appear as one unit to be seen to you.

At first you may feel like you are 'making shit up'(MSU) but we assure you that you just need to trust. You trust or you rust. If you get together with friends who are seers then often we will appear to all of you and you will all see us. This is again achieved through practice, practice, practice.

We often appear to children when they are young because they have no fixed ideas about what you should see and what you shouldn't — we don't like these fixed rules. Your social values and standards are crippling the young and the youths who do see things and your medical profession think you or the youths are crazy. In most cases you are not. *(The author is a clinician and has been witness to cases such as these. Having seen what they see.)* Trust, find another spiritual person if you can, find one and sit with them. However, there are a lot of 'wanna bes', it is worth asking around, at your local spiritual church or channelers around in the neighbourhood. In some districts you may have to travel out of town as these people often get ostracised especially when there are plenty of Zionistic religious factions that have strict rules which do not allow choice and information that doesn't serve their control of the masses.

We appear as you would expect, we always come with love and tranquillity unless we need to warn you then it will be more urgent. Feel in your teacher and master what it is. Unfocus your eyes just like in the aura teachings. If you think you are not seeing but another is, then perhaps more work in balancing your chakras or a daily 10 to 15-minute meditation would help. You all have five guides, and these may change throughout your life depending on what is coming up for you. Clairvoyance, health, direction/career, wealth and abundance, as well as gate keepers.

Different guides function at different stages in your life. Sometimes you only listen to one at a time in the beginning. This depends on your skill level and the contract you signed up for in this life. Different contracts are for different people.

Through meditation we can give messages, listen and observe with no ego and see what we send to you. Sometimes it can be through dreams, if recounting the dream or message just blurt it out don't think. We will be there to help you and to guide you to the right words. Keep the ego out as we will come through more strongly. We also come more to those who are following the path and are doing the best that they can, we understand when they fall off the path, everyone does, we smile; again, we do not judge you and we can see your true heart. You need not explain or justify anything to us — we already know everything. Trust, practice, egoless and non-judgemental elements are what we want you to strive for.

When we see you and you see us, we get connected more within the divine light, although you may not see it but the vibration of the molecules vibrating and resonating (4th dimension) so much that the naked eye can't see. However, the third eye sees it. The soul detects it and the heart sings.

We come to others for many different reasons for warnings, for blessings, for messages to the loved ones, with words of comfort and encouragement. We want you all to work together, with us, with each other and together we will make a difference. The world needs us and you to help save Gaia.

We see your seas getting more polluted and with dolphins and whales as your guardians you need to start there and we shall help. Not only with sounds and tones but also vibrations and love.

CLEAN UP THE SEAS, save the mammals and sea creatures. We will help, just ask.

Ask for guidance, ask for truth, ask for integrity in your governments, ask for yourselves and your children and our children. More enlightened beings, and light workers are being born and they will come up through the ranks and help lead in a gentle non-violent way. We are getting stronger with more support and acknowledgement.

We are not a figment of people's imagination, you are not M S U (Making Shit Up)... we trust you, you must trust us. Together we can save, change, renew, readjust all that is on this Gaia.

Ponder on this and practice, notice everything about your day, keep it happy and calm and things will be achieved without fuss or pain. If it is right, your day flows and you are listening to your heart and so then it will be as it should be.

We love you. Please go out there and help to show people that there are alternatives for all which doesn't have to be suppressed and curtailed for the greater good of the leader. There are some that don't come from a place of ego but sadly very few. Those will have great meetings and followers but others will dwindle and fall as the lack of integrity comes to light.

Love is in everything. We are love.

8.

Feelings
by Quan Yin

Today we want to talk to you about feelings. Feelings are the emotions that the master and teacher are expressing to the mind. Feelings can be used as tools in helping you to understand yourself and the vibrations of those around you. Feelings are generated from the deep core of your soul, and these are the lessons of the contract that you need to learn, how to harmonise and bring into line, your very being and nature.

Feelings cover states of anger, fear, sadness, joy, disgust and guilt. All these can give a feeling inside your very being. What we want you to do is observe these emotions/feelings and notice where they came from and why they happened. Feelings and processing these senses are part of your growing and being able to move on to the next contract. Without the understanding of these emotions/feelings you will be stuck and will have to understand them again, if not live through them again.

We want you to be able to sit in these feelings and understand them. You cannot just brush them off and move on. Things like traumas, bad events and upsetting instances cannot be swept under the carpet but instead they must be felt, just the feeling, do not relive the event that caused these feelings. It does not serve you to dwell on the actual event, these past experiences cannot be changed as nobody can turn back time. However, you can process them and learn from them so as not to repeat the experience again. In your mind's eye you can change the outcome of the feeling but not the actual event. If you keep having a flash of the event instead of feeling the fear or anger then change in your own mind how you would get out of that event. Change the outcome. But do this only if you cannot stop thinking the event through. If you can leave it in your stored memory then that is more serving. If you do have extreme feelings, again as we said sit in them, feel the emotion, not why it is there and then move on.

Part of the learning in the contracts is how to deal with human experiences. How to mature and learn to deal with these events. Remember you cannot get through this contract without some unpleasant event, nothing is sweetness and light all the time. Sure, you hear of people with charmed lives but remember things are never what they seem. If you see someone who you believe has got it all going on — trust us they haven't. Even these people have to work hard and feel the negative emotions that life brings them. Inside they may be feeling terrible but their persona doesn't allow anybody in to see their true self. We don't care how they look we just want you to learn from these events.

Sometimes there are events that you can't seem to be rid of, that keep coming back into the memory and dragging you down. Rumination and over thinking, does not serve you. If this event keeps coming up either change the outcome in your own mind or choose a really happy event as we have mentioned before, and smother the bad event with a good feeling and memory. Do not keep going over the bad event as this then keeps it in the memory banks and it will rear its head when you least expect it.

Even if you think you have done the work and therapy to get over these events this may not always be true. Years have gone by and you haven't even thought of it and then there is a trigger; it could be a phrase or a point of view or even a place, or a smell. Catch yourself when this happens and stop yourself from starting on the slippery slope to dwelling and rumination. You have a CHOICE. All humans have a choice. We want you to be happy and to process these human experiences. You have to learn.

The trial and error of your life makes you stronger and more capable in the long run. It enables you to serve mankind once you have completed all of your lives. We are with you all the way, remember to ask for help and support.

We want you also to notice when these feelings come up how they feel in your body. What reactions do you have? What does your sensory system feel? Does the feeling of disgust make you gag? What does anger manifest like in your body? Go through all these feelings—guilt, anger, fear, joy and sadness. If you notice these in your body, acknowledge them and then move it to a happy joyful state, you'll know when it is time to do so. Once you learn these soma sensory sensations in your body, then you can also use this skill to detect emotions in others through psychometry and crystals. The emotion will come off the object or crystal which gives you evidence of how they may have been feeling.

Writing to the person who has caused you angst or hurt can help with the residual emotions. Perhaps you just need to say something but not to that person as the social restraints and values do not want you to bare all of your emotions. And neither should you. It is not their stuff, it is yours. It is your contract not theirs. Do not drag things up from the past and confront them, it does not serve anyone. It is past and your job is to get over it and move on. It takes practice. Once you have written the letter and said everything you want to say, read it out loud and then burn it. We will deal with it and on a subtle energy level it will start clearing, you may even feel lighter.

Another part of becoming open and sensitive with your gifts is that often some people become too empathetic. This again does not serve anyone especially the empath. Other people's feelings are just that — other people's. Why take on other people's negative emotions? This is what empaths do. Perhaps wanting to wallow in other's self-pity. We observe that this does not serve anybody or any situation. It is not effective and helpful by doing this. Just because they want to feel and take off someone else's 'shit' and then wallow in the negativity — our question is why? Does the empath want to be a martyr? It's the other persons contract not the empath's. The outcome cannot be changed by the empath. Instead it wears the empath down, by getting sick and the negative emotion starts to affect processes of feeling and thinking. Nobody will thank the empath for taking on board other's negativity and feelings.

Another thing you have to be aware of is noticing feelings from others that you may feel are your own. Often, they are not, when you start opening, you will feel everything. It is a skill to start to discern yours from others. That is why it is imperative to process your emotional stresses and trauma to the body and the mind, then you can rest assured that you are clear of as much baggage as you can and then you can notice what isn't yours. This is a crucial time of growing and developing. It can be scary at first noticing other's pain and anxiety, but rest assured it is not yours. The skill is realising it is someone else's and choosing not to dwell, ruminate or catastrophise the emotion. Do not be dramatic. Those of you who walk the path do not get sucked into drama. Drama is emotion which comes from ego, this wraps you in vortexes of shit and emotions that the ego does not want you to ignore. The more drama and irrational behaviour there is, then more the ego has control. STOP IT, again it does not serve you. The ego holds on for longer than 24 hours yet the heart and soul let it go in this time and acceptance is found.

Think about it as a vortex of shit that you react to according to that emotion; anger – lash out; jealousy – punch somebody; fear – hurt someone. It is unlikely that happiness will have any detrimental affect but instead will end up laughing with them and sharing a moment, much more serving.

Remember:

ego — emotion

master/teacher — feelings

Learn to discern these feelings and emotions and learn how to care with detachment. Remember what these friends, family and acquaintances have written in their contract is their contract, not yours and you cannot 'fix' people or tell them how to process it. Instead it is about their learning and processing, they will learn. If not in this life but in the next.

We want you to be happy but you cannot truly witness happiness unless you have felt extreme sadness. Most people will feel this especially in the death of a loved one. This is hard but having faith and learning how to communicate with them or talk to them, knowing that they are around, will help. Grief is extreme and most people will experience it. It is difficult but we never said that these contracts and lives were a walk in the park. Living is about the long game, for you to experience so that you can assist more when you are on the other side of the veil after passing in order to help others.

Why do we want to have these experiences? Because it will make you a full angel and guide when it is your time to help. Know this and feel comforted that there is a bigger reason for these feelings and emotions and your experience of them.

Know that we love you and are your support when things get tough, ask for help and you will receive it but you should also keep your senses open to receive, and notice what is around you and we will send signs.

We love you so much and want to help.

And so it is…

9.

The Bigger Picture
by Arnoah

Hello, and so we are here again to help pass messages through to you that will help all of mankind. We wonder why often people are so cruel to each other. We come from a place of love and hope that you will too. We understand that for some, this is really hard. Especially if their upbringing has been violent and challenging. Unfortunately, this sets it up for the children to learn the wrong lessons. We think of the little children that are so cruelly worked and used for the profiteers to make their living. These children are not fulfilling their contract and as we observe these cruel and heartless people that are full of greed with no compassion. Unfortunately, they have strayed from their contract and are following their own free will, eventually they will suffer, not in the foreseeable future but when they get older and lonely and the soul will be suffering. We know life is hard and that was also your contract, the persecution of these child slaves, is not in their contract but they are the brunt of someone else's ego. The harder lessons in life are often set to be worked out in the adulthood of a person. This is where the suffering and learning takes place.

Sometimes we do not understand why these cruel people are doing this but sadly it is their upbringing and as very young souls they are getting the hang of living on this earth. New souls are being manifested all the time with the growing population as well as the population of other worlds. There is always choice and free will and we can only do so much to help the young ones. We cannot really interfere as we gave you choice and because of this there is no judgement. We are sorry that children suffer however they made that choice to be born in poverty-stricken areas, such as India and Philippines where there is cruelty to children.

Through generations, these things will gradually diminish, as we said before it takes generations to change thinking and new governments which will help strike out these terrible atrocities to children. Your children are here to teach the adults. Unfortunately, these adults do not stop to listen until it is too late and, in their contract, they more often than not end up in bad situation themselves or they get really sick and die prematurely.

Up here, there is peace and tranquillity. Many of you do not want to continue your contracts but this must be so, (To experience many many different situations.) otherwise you cannot help people for the greater good once you are through with your lives. To be their guides, to be their support when families go through a lot of tragedy. With faith, grief becomes easier and we would like to offer you as much help as you want but please ask, we cannot interfere or help unless you have given us your permission.

We look at the wider picture and for many generations so rest assured it will get better and gradually there will be less violence and hardship. Unfortunately, some religious sects are going to be harder to change as these top dogs are exactly that — dogs, and they only understand one thing — the placating of the ego. We are doing our best to help get rid of the higher leaders who do not serve humanity in a gentle way. We know organised religion can help many, and this serves them to lead a happier life but unfortunately some of the leaders are not ethically sound. Instead they rely on their own agenda and proclaim God - that is us, saying we agree with this. We have no judgement for them but we do not encourage it. If they believe they are doing the right thing at that time and that is the choice that they have made. Unfortunately, they take it too far, and with the adrenalin in ruling people, it becomes like a drug and they are not being their true authentic self. If they actually truly listened to their soul then they would not do this out of spite or meanness. They veer off their true path and let the ego take over. It takes over with all the drugs that make people aggressive, and the addictions that people continue, and that includes not only drugs, but also cruelty and the high it gives some people means they want to perpetuate the habit. We cannot interfere, instead we have to wait until they figure it out themselves by a turn of unfortunate events that happens to them or they die and learn the truth when they get here.

Jesus came from love. The Catholic and Christian church bases their teachings on love. It is unfortunate that man feels, in order to spread the word of God, they have to turn to bullying. Mohamed of the Muslim faith came from a place of warriorship, not from a place of love. As with everything, times and people's opinions start to skew the truth and change the words that we have tried to relay. Because it didn't serve them, and this life they should have stayed in poverty but instead suppressed and controlled others cruelly so that their wealth grew. We just wish that it is not monetary things that give you abundance but instead a rich and fulfilling life helping and seeing love, compassion and happiness. This is so much more sustaining and health is better. But do not give to the point of detriment of yourselves. You must find a balance and speak your truth if you cannot do things for others. Be kind and loving but not to the point of sickness to you. You are no use to anyone if you are sick and cannot continue on the amazing work that is set out in the contract and staying on the path.

We love you so much but you must listen to yourselves and take care of you in order to take care of Gaia.

Do not let resentment build up, this will make you sick as well. Know your boundaries and limitations. Be good to yourselves and when you need to rest and have space, then do so. Laughter is needed so much more so don't watch the news if it upsets you. Do things that make you happy so that you are more equipped and stronger to deal with unfortunate events that will happen. Don't be taken advantage of, be strong in who you are. Together we can teach others the way of love, it is easier for people to understand by demonstrations of kindness and they start to feel how good it is in helping others. If you have a good solid foundation of love and support then the grief, death, illness, and other experiences of that ilk will be easier to cope with.

We love you and so it is...

10.

Trust and Love by Archangel Raphael

And so it is...

We want to talk to you of trust and love...

This is a very fragile thing and can be broken easily, and may take some time to regain if it is lost and sometimes it doesn't come back at all. It is worth trusting that person if you feel okay about it but if your gut — teacher, feels it is wrong to do so then DON'T.

Trust is interesting, it is a word bandied about with the expectation that people just to do it. Unfortunately so many have ruined the word and the sense of trust that some people find it very hard to do. People treat others badly and abusively. Then they turn around and manipulate that person to use it against them "what don't you trust me — but I love you." This is a common phrase in abusive dynamics, and relationships. We feel that people band around the word love willy-nilly and this is not being authentic or genuine. Bad people or young souls use and abuse this word in order to get what they want. This is wrong and manipulative. Unfortunately, love can be misplaced and some feel that if they have been abused or mistreated when growing up then they have a false idea of what love should be.

Love is an interesting dynamic with some people. Love is non-racist, non-judgemental, only has vibrations of a high resonance, it makes you zing inside, it is unselfish if it is genuine. Many try to love unconditionally but this is a really hard path to take, younger souls on earth believe they have it sorted but often conditions come with it. We agree you should be cautious and not give love away if someone is going to take it and turn it against you. They are not on their path and contract; they are not listening to the master and teacher but only their ego.

We are love. Are you?

We stated before that there are different loves with children, family, partner and colleagues. Trust and love go hand in hand. With love comes trust, with trust comes love. We only want people to show kindness and love as well as consideration and compassion. This is a higher state of vibration.

You cannot keep giving love if it is not returned, it takes a very strong person to have that kind of love that continues to be given, and unconditional is very hard. We also suggest that you play with this idea and find out how you are with that.

Look at yourselves and question if you feel peeved that someone is only taking. Others will do this — those who sense your vulnerabilities and trust, be cautious, try giving and watch where it ends up. Do they reciprocate? Some may, but also, they may have an agenda in the end. It is up to you to figure and feel that out. Trust your instincts and your master, teacher which is connected to Source. We will not forsake you if you are asking the right question regarding someone.

With your skills that you are now honing this exercise will become quite automatic as you check in. With practice you will be able to discern this quite quickly. It is about trust… trust you, trust your gut, trust your higher self. How you do this is by taking a moment to birng your attention to what you feel in your heart. Then moving your attention to your gut or stomach, what do you notice? Perhaps, tingling, emptiness, wrenching, butterflies. You will know what to do if you pay attention to these signs.

With dynamics of relationships, trust is often given readily unless you have been hurt badly and this is a learnt lesson that your contract dictated. Genuine people offer trust readily until they have been let down emotionally or spiritually. This is a good way, but a hard way and you may need to get used to disappointments — especially if they are off their path. This is where the egos and the need for greed enters in, a "What's in it for them" mentality. If your trust is then thrown back in your face and the carpet ripped out from underneath then learn, look back at what your gut told you. Notice if you didn't follow it, how did you end up? Hurt and used? Now learn and learn fast. That is the best advice in this instant that we can tell you. Also, it takes a lot of guts to stand by your instinct when others may be trying to convince you to do what they want, for example lending money, signing a deal or giving them something. They may get angry, they may get moody with you and they may try to convince you that you are wrong. Stop take a moment don't be bamboozled.

This book is about learning to trust yourselves and the higher selves, it's about honing your skills and learning about the genuine and the false in all aspects. It's about living your soul's path and being AUTHENTIC. It takes a lot of strength and determination to stick to your guns. Gradually your friends and associates will start to change, as the non-genuine ones fade away so the authentic ones will gradually come in. This is the Law of Attraction. This is indisputable, it is a universal law. Mentioned by Buddha thousands of years ago " What you have become is what you have first thought". Other famous philosophers have also mentioned it, as well as in the bible, it just hasn't been called that specifically. (Birds of a feather flock together.) If you think or feel things in a happy state then happiness will continue. If you feel in a dark state then darkness will continue. If you are a happy person then you will attract other happy people and the same is for unhappy people. The term "Law of Attraction" was first printed in 1877 by the occultist Helena Blavatsky

The more you hang out with like-minded people so the numbers will grow, friends will change and the spread of love and trust will ensue.

The theme in this book is about you and helping people as well as yourselves in order to improve your quality of thinking, life, love, family and service. The more you think of how to flow through life, the more others will be attracted to you. Again, the Law of Attraction. Living an authentic life isn't the easiest, and the hard decisions may have to be asked, and followed. Once you have been practicing love, trust and authenticity then it will become easier. We have said this before practice, practice, practice. This is how it is. There will be a time when it becomes too hard and you just need a rest, that's fine, take a rest, consolidate your feelings, your energy and your love for mankind. You may feel spent and this is a sign that you are giving too much. Love and trust are a two way street. Genuine friends will not keep taking, genuine friends will give back, reciprocity — However if someone is still asking of you and not giving back analyse why you keep giving, if you are okay with this and it is not making you resentful and upset then that is fine. However, if you do not feel that this is okay, retract yourself, remember selfish people keep coming back as a subtle bully, you may not realise it at first and then the emotional blackmail creeps in, notice this.

Any genuine friend that has equal passing of energy between you will not do this. But someone who is not genuine, who is selfish (Selfishness; doing what they want, where they want, how they want, when they want.) and out only for their immediate gain will make you feel like shit.

However, you are responsible for your own feelings, nobody else is, you can choose to feel guilty for no known reason and kowtow to their selfishness, you are responsible.

Look at the situation objectively, would you ask this of someone, would you push until your friend breaks, would you mirror this ungenuine person's behaviour and if you did would it make you feel good. If the answer is 'probably not' then extract yourself from that dynamic and choose what is right for you. If it is right for you, then you're genuine, with love and trust friends will not chastise or judge you but instead will honour your decision and respect you for being authentic to the master and teacher. They will understand and accept this unconditionally. The not so understanding may become dramatic, and emotional, using the ego to drive it. Walk away. Ask for help from us and we will help — perhaps not at first but remember we work on many different levels and we have the long picture in our sights, so trust us and we will deliver. Trust or you Rust. Trust us, trust yourselves, trust your friends that are genuine, trust your authenticity. You are amazing and beautiful if you come from a place of love and trust.

Be who you truly are, not what the ego is telling you but what your master and teacher is teaching you. Check in with yourself for practice when meeting new people, check in with them in an energetic feel, what do you notice, gather information about people and your relationship with them, be it business, professional, or personal. Start building up a repertoire of your observations, somatosensory and gut feelings. Start discerning one from another. Experience and practice.

We love you always and unconditionally, you must learn this and feel this and trust this.

Until next time, go with love…

11.

Challenges and Questions by Arnoah

We want to talk to you of challenges and questions that people will try to either learn or catch you out; or so they think. It is hard to catch someone out if they come from a genuine place of love and authenticity.

You will feel the ones who are challenging; this is a good thing. The more people challenge the more the word of integrity and authenticity will spread. By using your gifts to help people, so the sceptics will see that there is more than either of you can prove through science.

Remember, we are with you, call us in and rest assured that we will be behind you. Open up your nothingness and sit with what you feel. If they are genuine and want to find out more then take your time, clear your energy. Use the pillar of light technique to protect yourself. For example: Plant your feet on the ground, imagine and connect with Gaia beneath your feet. Visualise the ground connecting with the soles of your feet. Allow the Gaia energy to come up through your body to the eighth chakra. This is about 15 cm above your head. If you focus on this space above your head you can sometimes feel energy or tightness, a breeze, or a coolness on the top of your head, this is the seventh chakra communicating with the eighth — the higher self, the one that communes with us more than the third eye, (sixth chakra). There is more of a sense of calm from the eighth. We can communicate and translate for you the messages that we need to give. And please as ever leave your own baggage at the door of nothingness. Have no preconceived ideas about what you should and shouldn't say to people. Remember, they asked and gave you their permission. Answer their questions with love.

With the clearing of your own baggage it should be easier to move into the nothingness and wait for responses. This can take several minutes, and the person should be told that this can take some time. It will become easier once you have practiced a lot. It's a bit like learning how to drive, and you are stuck at a junction and the traffic is building up behind you and you start to get more nervous. You miss the space in the moving traffic and you can feel the cars behind you get impatient. Remember that you need to calm yourself down, breathe and then find the gap in the traffic. It is the same when channelling messages for these people. The ones that do not hassle and goad you are the ones that will give you space and acceptance to help you hone your skill. Others will make you nervous — but these are your feelings, not theirs and therefore you can control them. So do so. Be strong in who you are and breathe. You have done the work, now it is confidence and trust in us and yourself.

Sometimes these people will also challenge you on your belief system and they will ask you difficult questions: be sure of who you are and confident that we are behind you.

Others will ask you about poverty, and child abuse, we have answered that one. Others will ask of war. This is a predicament that you humans have manifested in order to satiate greed and powered up egos. In some respects, the leaders who claimed to look after their people called on them to defend their borders and we get that. It's about preserving the culture, tradition and perhaps faith. Really, do you think we want you to kill for us? NO, NO, NO, NO. There are always other ways.

Men take our name in vain; it gives them just reasons to take over other countries. This is not necessary as humans can live in synergy with Gaia and each other. Technology has made war very scary and instant. The testing of nuclear weapons that is not necessary and is followed by a large ego. There are countries — USA, UK, and other European countries that help defend the others from the invading power/ego. It is possible that all of the world can live in their own countries and they will be sustained with the growth of produce and exporting. But it is unfortunate that there are the egos that rape and pillage their land (Zimbabwe). They don't care about their essential workforce. However, they forget that they (the leaders)are just as important as these farmers and other workers which are vital in sustaining the country and smooth running of it. We want the leaders to put in place education about how to be self-sufficient. We like the trading of produce and things, when there was no money. Then money came in as an energy source. This energy source of money became more and more important, and has bought them beautiful things but sadly they do not see the beauty in everything around them. Instead they are selective and greedy. More and more so in the political and corporate realms. There are those who give back but these are in the minority.

As we have said before the gentle removal of those egotistical leaders driven by greed will eventually happen, they will die — this is the law of nature and circle of life. They will be gone eventually and rest assured this is when the new generations will step up and fight for their people. There will still be hidden narcissists but they will eventually be exposed and moved on.

There are souls here and now that are a lot older who will help this come to fruition. The new born and young children are our new Gods and Goddesses and these will start the new loving order. There is a way of not fighting to work out our differences. We would like the world leaders if they have a problem with another to put boxing gloves on if they must fight and battle it out in a ring. That way only one person suffers not all the others, the costs are brought down and life is not spent or wasted. There are of course other ways but men being men like to battle it out somehow. If all else fails then this may be the last resort. There is chess of course, which may serve better; skill, strategy and ultimately a battle of wits.

It is unfortunate that the leaders don't want to put their life on the line but are happy to use others. Yes, war is good for one thing — population control. If you looked at it from that perspective it would have needed to happen.

Instead, approach war from a place of love, looking after everyone, having very little greed, and small egos. Then love for the less fortunate and helping them may make people realise that they can't keep having off-spring, especially if they (earth, cities, and families) cannot take care of the children as the environment is not always ideal. To be able to have access to clean running water, good employment and health care and enough food to go around. Collective consciousness is needed. You don't have to lose yourself for the greater purpose, but instead invent and design a way to show how unique you are. Work with others and treat them as you would expect to be treated.

We wish everyone thought this way as we are sure some of the world leaders would not want to go to their own prisons; live themselves in poverty-stricken areas or in their prisons. We know this will change; we know these things take time.

People will ask you why there is so much suffering; this and the other Big Picture essays in chapter 9 will help your answers.

There is enough land on this earth to sustain all of you. However, the chemicals that are being fed into this earth are destroying it. There has to be more sustainable practices with organics in order for Gaia to truly recover. Companies that genetically modify plant seeds to combat disease but cannot germinate to make new crops and therefore farmers having to buy back more seed. This is not self-sustaining. This is money and ego driven by individuals and or biochemical companies. Be warned. In time this will also diminish, as we have said before those who stray off their path and contract will eventually come to a sticky end. Perhaps they will think about what they have done as well as the damage to Gaia that has been done. If they realise this in time then they will not have to work it out in another life. However, if they don't, they will come back and suffer until they learn that the ego isn't the be all and end all.

Stop screwing with the ecosystem, leave out the chemicals, learn to trust and love each other or at least treat with respect and acceptance. You have a saying "all good things come to those who wait." This can happen with global community and Fair Trade. We can see and feel that there are humanitarian workers that are doing their best at ground level; they are to be congratulated. In the end these humanitarian people will make it up the ladders of these cooperates, political parties, and associations to eventually make a difference. They will be excellent at this as they have seen what it is like on ground level. It will come.

This is how it will be… so it is… we love you all.

12.

Guides and Loved ones, Past Lives by Quan Yin

And so it is… we want to talk to you today of guides and loved ones. Loved ones know all things about you. They understand when you call them in, what it is that you would like help with. They are your loved ones that are connected to the family either through blood or through marriage and close friends. That's not to say a distant connection with someone isn't there. The passed loved ones and guides can help the weirdest connection; for example, they may help to orchestrate a meeting between two of you for a greater purpose. It may happen in the strangest way, so expect the unexpected with these beautiful spirits. The connection is deep but you may not realise that you may have spent many other lives with them; just not necessarily in this life.

Loved ones once passed often need to go off and mend themselves, either physically or emotionally. This means that if they suffered from a stroke so the energy of that healing has to take place to make the energy orb (within the soul) whole again. Or if happened in a bad accident so the physical trauma must be mended as this is still part of the orb — the energy orb of the soul. Emotional trauma can be harder to get over than physical trauma. The soul or orb has to process and work from emotions to feelings and lessons learned to become whole again. This is like life as well, deep, unseen wounds are far harder to process, to truly let go.

Physically, deceased loved ones choose how to appear, as discussed before. These loved ones know about very important parts to your life and accept that you may not have made the best decisions for yourself. If in an abusive relationship, things will seem harder. People give you advice, such as to leave the abusive partner, but often they have an emotional hold over you; either through the abusive partners own insecurity, low self-esteem or general negativity. It takes someone with resilience who can dig deep to get out of such a relationship and unhealthy dynamics.

Deceased loved ones are always there as soon as you call or they may just want to hang out to make sure you are okay and sometimes they want to warn you of an accident or hurt. They can't necessarily change the outcome but they can help make it less harmful, especially if this is written into your contract. You still have to feel pain in some aspects, but the loved ones can reduce the hurt or permanency of the injury. They love you. we love you.

Reincarnation:
This is the process by which the soul comes onto Gaia to learn lessons good and bad in order to develop and refine the art of living. We can have many, many, many lives if you are a slow learner or just a few if you have learnt quickly. Some of the Ascended Masters decide to sample life. They know this is harder than up in Source, and sometimes the ascended masters like a challenge. St Germain has come down recently — just over the last 14 years and is living through life. The new warriors and healers are coming back more.

There are some memories; the more progressed lives are more likely to remember some things, that is how Buddha is chosen. The way that humans select the next Buddha is by going around to many villages and testing the new children to see if they are the next Buddha reincarnate. A selection of objects from the previous Buddha is gathered and other ordinary household items that the Buddha may have used. The objects include some of his childhood toys from the previous life, it could be a pen, or a toy or even just a book that was precious to the last Buddha. In total there are generally 20 items that the boy or girl needs to identify to show that they are the true Buddha reincarnate. When the children are tested by the elders, they note what was picked by the child. If they get it all correct all 20 of their own personal items (there are about 40 items in total) then they are taken away to start studying the scriptures and will be groomed and taught by the elders to become the next Buddha. There have been over 10,000 Buddhas to date and this is a tried and tested way of the selection of the new Buddha.

Others will have a sense of familiarity and comfort when in the presence of something familiar or something which has been in their lives beforehand. It is possible to find out about your last lives, but remember they are in the PAST and should have no bearing on your life now. Learn from them. There may be a reason why you are drawn to this particular trait or profession. Some of you will gravitate towards each other because of past lives together, it could be to right wrongs from the past, or learn how to get on with this person, and the lesson of this dynamic needs to be learnt and stabilised rather than remaining erratic, and/or dramatic. If you feel you have a relationship dynamic or issue in this life, then look at it. What rubs you up the wrong way, do you grate on each other's nerves? How can you ever be in the same room as each other? This is the lesson of the contract that perhaps needs to be solved. A simple explanation is that you could have been on opposing sides in a war and you came up against each other on the battlefield. Whereas if you feel comfortable and are a good team either at the office or on the field then perhaps you have been brothers in arms. There are many explanations as to why people have certain relationships and lives together.

Sujith and Sammy
Born in Sri Lanka (formerly Ceylon), Sujith was barely old enough to speak when he began to tell his family of a previous life as a man named Sammy. Sammy, he said, had lived eight miles to the south in the village of Gorakana. Sujith told of Sammy's life as a railroad worker and as a dealer of a bootleg whiskey called arrack. After an argument with his wife, Maggie, Sammy stormed out of his house and got drunk, and while walking along a busy highway was struck by a truck and killed. Young Sujith often demanded to be taken to Gorakana and had an abnormal taste for cigarettes and arrack.

Sjuth's family had never been to Gorakana and hadn't known anyone that fit Sammy's description, yet, being Buddhists, were believers in reincarnation and therefore not completely surprised by the boy's story. Investigations, including one conducted by a professor of psychiatry at the University of Virginia, confirmed as many as 60 of the details of the life of Sammy Fernando who indeed had lived and died (six months before Sujith's birth), just as Sujith had said. When Sujith was introduced to Sammy's family, he surprised them with his familiarity with them and his knowledge of their pet names. This is one of the strongest cases of reincarnation on record. https://www.liveabout.com/the-mystery-of-past-life-recall-2596293

Past life regression doesn't always serve people. What's in the past should be left in the past unless you are mentally stable enough to look at it objectively and learn. Ensure that you are not the sensitive type that takes past lives on board. This is not necessary, and that is why they are past.

Meditation for past lives:
Sit comfortably and relax. Breathe in and out deeply; in through your nose and out through your mouth. Allow your breath to settle. Bring your attention to the third eye area. See a nothingness and allow that to envelope your energy. Notice yourself walk in the nothingness, and through to a gap in the absence of light. Move through that gap and you see a forest, move through the forest and into a field, and a path. Follow that path to the big house. Notice how splendid the house is, how welcoming. Open the bold front door, stand in the centre of the hall way. You see a grand staircase going up to another level. Breathe. Turn and move to the room on left, *what do you see*? Settle into that room, look about you, notice what furnishings there are, what kind of clothes you are wearing. What is on the walls or about your life in that time. *If a scene of this life appears watch and observe, this will give you clues or situations you may have been in previously*. When you have felt the need to move — do so. Out of that room and into the opposite room. Perhaps pausing in front of the staircase, *Has it changed?* go to the room… *what do you see?* Look again all around you may even notice smells. Sit in the room, *what kind of chair and table?* All of these give you clues. Remember to breathe. When you feel you have noticed enough come out to the hall. The doors will close. *Has the staircase changed again or the same?* Turn and exit the house and down the path. Through the forest and up to the opening of the nothingness – the absence of light. Breathe and relax some more. To bring yourselves back to the here and now, breathe deeply again, feel your fingers and toes, gradually breathing new

oxygen to the whole body. Relax and come back gently. Write down what you saw, noticed and observed in the environment of those rooms. Thank your soul for the information and the guides for protecting you on your journey. Amen

Past lives will turn up in the rooms, the things you see will give you clues of what your profession was. If you do this several times you may find out more and more.

If you are having problems with career choices this may be a useful exercise. Or if you want to find out about a person in your work space then this may be helpful too.

Thank you.

13.

Compassion
by Arnoah

We are here today to talk to you about compassion and what it really means. Some people are half hearted when it comes to compassion. This is a state of mind where you think of the other no matter how they look, no matter what they have done before and their history, with no judgement. Compassion is an offshoot of love and how it manifests is through the kindness that is unrequited, the love that keeps supporting you in the hour of need. To have unbiased compassion be really hard to obtain. It means taking your own baggage, prejudices and racism out of the picture. Also, do not go back to the old events that have a bearing on your life now. With those past hurts it can take away the true meaning of compassion, especially if you cannot let them go. Compassion is hard to truly accomplish; it is unselfish, it is gentle and supportive. When helping someone keep the other personal interpretations, experiences and influences out of it. Be with that person. If you have no words of comfort then just being with them will help on one level. Use the skills that you have been honing and move the good, golden, loving energy around them… move it around like warm blanket. Allow them to calm down if they are angry or frustrated. Try not to offer your opinion as this may aggravate them. Ask open questions and just let them talk. They need to figure it out themselves. If offering advice be objective, look at both sides of the story. Opinions tends to be subjective if they ask yours, and one sided. Do not bring prejudice into the conversation. Just be with them. If they have experienced trauma, be careful and hold the space. What this means is to be in your own mastered power, don't give it away but instead be a supporting energy. They have to go through these learning episodes in life and it is up to you to allow their journey to be unhindered and the lessons that they need to learn be learnt. You cannot take away the hurt. Hurt often happens when the truth has been spoken and they do not like what has been said. They need to learn from it. If it is an offense that they feel, then they must process this. So if you are the person that is hurting, firstly look at yourself. Go within, look at the way it has affronted you. Why is that? Is it disparaging to your culture, to your family or to yourself? The biggest lesson to learn is as we have said before ACCEPTANCE. Acceptance of them, acceptance of what they have been through, cruel or otherwise. There is no good and bad, it is just their experience and contract. Hurt is something which is hard to understand and accept at first.

Look at the reason that you are hurt or they are hurt. You may feel this way if you are still dealing with your emotions. It's about caring with detachment. Listen to them; hear the stories of the person. Work through the events that they are hurting with. Explain from different perspectives what could happen to others and their point of view, allow them the space and time to process this and then the compassion will come once everything is dealt with. There should be no regrets in your life, this enables you to listen with compassion too. If you are following your soul — teacher and us then the event that you're working through, making the right decision at the time for yourself of that moment. If you have chosen from your heart and soul then the decision will be the right one. So no regrets will be felt.

People start feeling guilty when they haven't been true to themselves. Will often put that on you or another unsuspecting person. The emotion of guilt can suck you in to a vortex of negative emotion. Try not to get stuck in the emotion; notice and look at how it manifested and where it came from?

War is also based on feelings of guilt to have to fight for their country. A leader wants what is best for him and his country (we hear him say as there aren't that many females ruling). As we said before, leaders have an ego, otherwise in this day and age they would not get to the top as it is still the old paradigm of power and egos. By invading another country, they aim to get more for their countrymen. However, the people probably don't need or want any extra land. Then the leader will start speeches by playing on the guilt or the drive of the people.

Giving them empty promises to get what they themselves want. Using patriotic feelings and pride in their homeland. Join up, kill people so that you may have a better land for you and your family.

Really, all they are doing is playing on those guilty feelings.

Wanting the best for their families but what is actually happening is the leader is lining his pockets, lining his own family's pockets to get the best all for them not necessarily the real countrymen.

Voting is the people's way of getting what they want but never really seeing change. Immediate change is not apparent but in the long run over decades your voting will matter. Ideals take time to change in the government. For example, equal rights were demonstrated long before it became law. Unfortunately, corruption is at the very top and this filters down to anyone who needs, wants or has power.

Your leaders show very little compassion — only now are some coming up through the ranks but at the moment the top powers are starting to corrupt those new and energetic people. The new political leaders of tomorrow can be influenced in their careers but once in those senior positions then their philosophies and ideas in helping the world will come through.

When you come across people who need your help and support, before you judge them remember you can never imagine where they have been before and what experiences they have been through. They also may not tell you the full story. It is not yours to know, just listen and treat them with compassion and support. This is again about clearing your baggage in order to be compassionate. You are not judge and jury. You are not the one to make a decision about who to help but instead get the collective new movement going to assist Gaia is a start. This is a long and slow process but you all can help, be mindful and have fun.

Listen with integrity to those who you help and you will probably not know the whole story but that is fine. As we said before it is not yours to know.

With practice, your compassion, acceptance, and having no judgement will develop. However, you need to love yourself in order to do this work. Clear your shit. The hurts, the emotions, so you grow and learn. Meditation regularly will certainly help and just do it…

Compassion is a hard thing to totally get a handle on, you have to sit in it and feel it yourself. And for those of you who are not good at receiving you have to receive compassion from others to truly feel what it is like. It is the purest form of giving; parcels and presents are just surface.

What we notice is when someone starts to truly feel they have received real compassion with acceptance then they are more able to give compassion. Accept that you deserve this from others. You as light workers have a propensity to give, give and give and you forget to receive, or you think it is wrong and selfish to get from others. In order to give YOU MUST RECEIVE. This is often a really hard lesson to learn for you givers. By learning to love yourself so you will be able to receive love from others. It is your right to receive love, you are deserving, everyone is deserving of love. If you feel a person is not deserving, then you are wrong. Everybody has that right. If you feel they do not, then give it anyway and they will feel the difference between love and hate or anger. It will soften them and show them the way. Perhaps they may start listening to their soul and teacher, but if they do not that is fine too. Give love and you will receive love. Not necessarily from that person but from others; perhaps those you least expect it from. This is the karmic cycle. This is the giving and receiving aspect of life. The flow of energy, the flow of experience and feelings.

If you work with us towards a more compassionate world then Gaia will survive. Slow change is a more permenant change than something quick and radical. It's like cramming for an exam, you will forget it within days but if you slowly learn the material, then it will sink in and become part of you and your knowledge. It is the same with compassion and love, the more you learn and experience it the more it will become entrenched into your very being. You will ooze love and compassion, your aura will change you will have a shining light behind you and more and more people will gravitate towards you. Be warned people will want what you have, preserve yourself and hang out with other like-minded people that can nurture you. This will empower you to go out and help the more struggling, the more desperate of people in your life; be it in the office, on the milk runs or in the factories. We are behind you as you learn to show more integrity, more love and more compassion. We are smiling again, this is beautiful that so many want to learn, we thank you for this and the good work. You will fall down or trip up but notice that the ego is creeping in and to recognise this, accept that it wants a voice. Listen to the emotion it's trying to get out of you; notice, observe and then feel, the ego won't stand a chance.

We want you to observe others and how they do this practice, we want you to tune in to feel and see their energy, you will start to see patterns and waves around others, defocus, it will be, and remember no judgement or prejudice.

And so it is …

14.

Growth
by Melchizedek

Growth within and without. Growth within yourselves is paramount and we want you to look and enable yourself to look without prejudice of yourself. We want you to see yourself for who you truly are, warts and all. To see you as a mean person at times when certain acts weren't necessary. Just a vicious attack; it's okay. Everyone has bad thoughts but you need to recognise what they are and what they represent or stand for. Why do they come up? Do you feel usurped? Disgruntled? And you want to attack a person verbally or physically? It's fine. Everyone has some bad thoughts at some time in their lives. Can you control it or do you act on it? If you do act out you need to understand why? Is it an eye for an eye? But then where will that stop, that is the beginning of many wars. Before you do retaliate, look at how that will serve you and the loved ones around you. Instead go inside, feel the anger perhaps go for a run or walk up a hill. Get rid of the anger in a more constructive way. Feel it on the inside, sit in it and then let it get diluted in the nothingness. By moving through these episodes, there is growth on the outside and inside. Learn why and how it happened and don't let anybody push those buttons again. Deal with it. Accept it. Growth on the inside is about raising your vibration through experiences and feeling. Learning from these experiences so we grow, mature and begin to understand the knowing.

Change is inevitable inside and out. Once you are looking after the teacher and master so look after your temple, the body. Try to look after the environment that you live in to give them a fighting chance in this polluted Gaia. Once you have mastered that and are growing in mindfulness and awareness of the surroundings then look at growing your own produce if you don't already. Be it herbs in a pot on the kitchen windowsill or a beautiful garden. These are very therapeutic. Looking after your environment means that you nurture and grow yourself. Feeling the energy of the plants as they grow can be a useful exercise if you haven't already experienced that. Through experiences with feelings so souls grow, through good food and water the soul can also be nurtured. This can stave off disease and other unnecessary afflictions that haven't been written into your contract. Keep yourself healthy in the body and the mind will also stay so. This includes exercise and fresh air.

Connect with others, grow your friendships with kindness and compassion. Keep in touch with family and see how they grow. Nurturing others will help to nurture yourself. To grow wise and accepting of all. This is true growth of human lives

The world that you live in is going through huge amounts of growth and change. This is inevitable, as the world powers change through the decades so their ideals and philosophies do too. They look to grow their pockets, their storage of material goods as if they can use all 20 cars at once, really? Sometimes growth is misconstrued as wealth. Then wealth becomes a dirty word. Especially if in the wrong hands. Mankind can live on an average wage and standard of living. If you shared all the wealth around the world it would even out and everyone would have the same. But it is the power that goes with wealth and then both grows. Misappropriate use of wealth is sad but a reality. Through decades and cycles of generations things will alter and grow, including the population, so things need to adjust and make way for more adequate living.

The control of growth will have to happen around the Earth and the materials that are being used will have to change especially if they are going to continue to grow woods and forests for manufacturing and houses. The eco-environment must be monitored carefully as the equilibrium will be upset and growth will develop in the non-self-sustaining direction.

Watch the environment, watch how others grow and discover. Through your actions of using energy work, guidance through cards, healing with stones and working with us and interactions with others, so by noticing your actions your friends will grow and learn themselves. All to the greater good and understanding of whom and what you are.

Part of the big picture is growth and understanding of your soul. To grow in acceptance and non-judgement in your soul and in lives that you have is paramount. Growth is everything. The more people understand about true compassion the more it will save Gaia. Look within to become without — without prejudice, without judgement without hatred, without anger without jealousy.

And so it is…

15.

Lives
by Arnoah

We want to talk to you about lives, how there are many, many lives that you have to live to help you learn about all aspects of the human condition. You will notice how different people react to different circumstances and different situations.

Think about how people react to a scenario. In an office, factory or other workplaces some can be thinking of only the here and now, as well as what they want, not what they need. Others will have a wider perspective, what others need before themselves. There are different states of mind and different states of progress through your different lives. There is a hierarchy of progressive lives and reincarnation.

There are many who are on their middle lives and young lives through the reincarnation process. The older ones, especially the light workers amongst you are closing in on your last lives, some are even on the last now.

Ever wondered why you couldn't understand a way a colleague is working and figuring out issues and problems at work the way that they do. To you it seems incomprehensible — why on earth do you think they reacted that way? It could be that they are on an early life cycle and that there are fundamental lessons to learn now before they can move on to the next. The people who are wiser, or seem to be, don't react so quickly to things and instead they are calmer and steadier even when it comes to a crisis at work.

Sages and warriors are on this earth at the moment and there is a process by which mankind comes onto this earth, then slowly moves to your chosen profession. People often gravitate towards the professions that they have done on this earth before. It could be several or a few. It just depends on what you wrote into this contract. Before you repeat and are born there is a discussion with yourselves — your soul and the ascended masters and teachers. You have a get-together to talk about and feel what would be right for you. What you have been through before, what you have learnt and how you will build on the skills and growing of your soul through this next life. It is openly discussed with you and the events and situations that you have learnt by. We ask you questions as in an interview and we discuss the best way to move forward into the next life. We talk about where you want to experience the things that you need to and work out the best place to learn those lessons.

The younger souls don't have so much experience so at the early stages they are not sure about what questions to ask as they don't have a catalogue of events and experiences to draw from. Think of it this way — it's like leaving school and going to university. When you first start learning a subject that you know nothing about; you ask questions about what is going on in the lecture and you realise that in fact there was no need to ask the question as it was covered later in the lesson. You don't have enough knowledge to know what to ask. It is like this with life. In the beginning you do not have enough skill and experience to know where to best learn the lessons of the soul and human extremes. We help you in the beginning and you have to trust us that we know what is the best way to begin on the journey. What we find is that in the beginning the soul will often go to a desperate country with poverty and strife. Through this early suffering it teaches a great first lesson on deprivation and cruelty. Through these experiences, because they are exactly that — experiences, what you notice is that the younger souls are often out for themselves as they do not trust ANYONE. Their lives and experiences are built on fear... they often mistrust people, some however don't trust anyone. Then there are the souls who trust everyone. This too is a state that is perhaps not ideal as they will get ripped off, taken advantage of and used as much as possible. If this is happening and you can see it happening and you are okay about it, then that is fine. What we can say is often this person is on their last life or lives and they have mastered the art of unconditional love. They are the ones that understand how the younger ones operate and through the exploitation of yourself that alone may give them a lesson. Karma is useful in these cases, as an abuser of power that takes and takes from people, as we have said before, will come back again or later in that life and suffer for their bad behaviour. That is exactly what it is, bad behaviour. We only observe that these young souls will learn when we put things in their path that will try to teach them about compassion, kindness and reciprocity. Then if that doesn't work, and they take no clues from what we are trying to teach then a big serious open discussion when they have completed that life will be on the cards.

As you work through your lives, we trust that the soul learns, and from the chats that we have in Source then the lessons and experiences will be slowly learned. You can have many tens to hundreds of lives, especially if the soul is a slow learner. However, as you go through them so the soul picks up speed in the learning of the lessons.

So, how to deal with the younger souls in the workplace; if people frustrate you then look beyond what you see. How do they tick, are they coming from a place of insecurity, low self-esteem, perhaps they are in an abusive relationship and this is the only way they can assert themselves as the bully is at home and the work place is the only place that they can feel valued or heard. However, it is unfortunate that other colleagues may not see this, and react quite badly to them. Have compassion and an inquiring mind as to why they are like this. It could also be that you have shared a life with them before and karma is being worked out with you two in this life.

Other scenarios of this kind are that other wrongs between you have happened before and, in this life, it is to be worked out and dealt with. It takes a strong soul to confront and have a frank discussion with that colleague and perhaps after that the relationship or dynamic will shift to a better understanding. However, do be warned that this can back-fire depending on how far they may have wandered off their path. If this is the case then the ego has taken over for a while. Often the younger souls have this battle for many lives but eventually through meditation and discipline the ego gets suppressed and the heart and soul start to blossom.

Older souls tend to gravitate towards gentler professions. Such as professors, judges, painters, healers and teachers. Older souls can move up through the ladder as great leaders and don't let their ego speak too often but instead look at the bigger picture for the gain of humanity not the gain of their own ego. At the moment of the world leaders there are quite a few young souls ruling; especially in Africa. These will eventually pass on and will live an interesting returned life. They too will sample the suffering and poverty that they have caused. So, if you have this belief then the knowing will help and give you confidence in the process and that your life will only get better.

The Hindu faith relies heavily on this process of karma and reincarnation. What we have noticed is that the Hindu people in poverty are happy about where they are at in their lives cycle that if they suffer in this one then they will surely go on to the next one with a far better contract. This doesn't always happen especially if they have exploited others in these poverty-stricken areas. The religious men — the Brahmans have implied and suppressed the poor and contrived a caste system in India. We agree they have got it right regarding the reincarnation but they have taken advantage of the system and used it to their own ends. Gandhi who is now an Ascended Master believed in equality and not the caste system. He fought against this in his life on earth.

What started out to be living the true word of Source then got twisted around for their own gain. We also do not understand why women in some countries are treated as a lesser citizen; all souls are equal, really, they are, all souls are equal, and should be treated accordingly. Sure, there are some that understand the workings of the system and the universe better than others but the actual soul is still the same. The differences are that they have learnt more lessons, had more lives, and have grown spiritually. There are different levels of this, those who are just beginning to understand, and that will be who read this book. We want you to hone your skills and to teach others.

There are different learners who are at different stages of their education. We encourage you to ask, seek and learn new skills. You will be directed to the path or skill that you need to learn. Gradually over many lifetimes those skills will be stronger and more potent. That is the difference between amazing healers and the ones who are just beginning. Those amazing healers are often on their last life or close to it. However, some of you chose to come back to help more of mankind as you feel you can do more work down there. Others who have completed are happy to stay at Source and continue the work from here. Once the contract is completed then you come back to Source to talk to us about the next episode that needs to be learnt.

Once at Source you will start to understand what all this is about and how we can help those left on this earth. Those who have strayed from their contract and have left their path will have many more lives to experience until they have figured it out; learn to be good to others, and to show compassion. To help others without prejudice, and of course, acceptance.

It is sad that many operate from fear in their lives, and low self-esteem. The self-absorbed people that you work with will be wary of those of you who are more evolved. By this we mean that they have discovered that they are not the be all and end all of everything, and your world is not changing for them. This can be a hard lesson to learn and many fight this. The wiser understand that everyone has lessons to learn; good and bad. A lot more knowledge comes to those who notice the mistakes that they have made. Or the wrong call and how it affects them, their soul, their heart and their ego. Noticing what is happening in their body, the soma sensory feelings and effects in the body. Those who find stillness when all those around are running around like headless chickens. Notice those who are too fast in life to notice others and their feelings, or their energy. People often feel threatened by someone who goes through life with deliberation and quietness. They feel (on a level they may not be aware of) that you as a calm light worker or budding light worker move through space differently. This can be threatening because you are different. We are thankful to those who do work in offices who help show the other younger souls how it is and show them how to operate without a hidden agenda. We like visibility, we like that the truth is being said. If only more corporates would actually follow this line of thinking. However, this cannot always be done as others in the office can feel threatened and undermined by their inexperience. They will often feel your power and not know why you feel different. The auric field of those who are working with us will feel strong and empowered. Sure, you will fall off the wagon, but you also need to. What is useful when you do is noticing how you feel within yourself. Do you feel out of sorts? Can't quite put your finger on what is going on? Perhaps you start getting sick, numerous colds, or develop an auto immune problem. Notice these things and ask yourself why? What have you missed, or not seen? Things in life aren't flowing, feel as you have to force a situation, to make it happen. If this is the case stop rushing, stop forcing the flow. Relax, allow things to happen and sit back and notice how the body feels this way.

We advise that if you begin to feel this, try to meditate more, hang out with like-minded people, get back on your path. Elevate your vibration, raise your centred happiness and smile more often. Eat good foods, happy meat, fresh produce and fewer additives. Start becoming in tune with your physical body — it can tell you volumes of what is going on. You can do this by relaxing into a meditation and slowly work through your body from the toes and work all the way up to your head including the crown chakra. Notice in each body part how it feels. The body's cells have an emotional memory and if practiced can tell you what is happening. Work through all your muscles, limbs, organs and structures. What do you feel? Pain, emotion, energy, stillness or anything else? If there are memories being held in your body, notice which emotion it is and sit in it. By that we mean feel, experience and notice that emotion, it could be anger, frustration, jealousy or another state. Close your eyes and be. Hold the nothing space with that emotion. It may at first get worse before it starts to diminish, which is okay and normal. Once you feel it is diminishing and is not so intense then allow it to move off. The feelings will gradually get diluted and washed away. Another layer of ego and events moving off. (Peeling back the layers like an onion.) This signifies that you are getting closer to Source and closer to completing the lives and karma.

Remember, also that a useful tool of those of you who are more evolved is to move your happy energy around those who are being shitty and unreasonable. Do not judge as they may be quite warranted about their misgivings on this matter as they come from a different place than you. They have had different circumstances in growing up, different parents and different stresses. All you can hope for is that this is a life lesson of their contract not that they have strayed off the path including being 'out for anything they can get for themselves no matter who is standing in their way.'

This is where the trust comes into it and the belief of the bigger picture that you cannot fully comprehend. And you are not meant to until your work is done on this earth. Like work where the bosses don't tell staff everything and full visibility is not happening. We do not allow you to know everything as this can be too big for the human mind to understand. We come from a bigger space than you can ever imagine. Also, some of you are not ready to hear all. It's about stages and lives and how far you have progressed depends on the information that we give you. The human mind can be very fragile and too much for the human condition to take on board.

We only withhold information because your soul is not ready to hear, unlike bosses holding back information for fear of losing the job or stability or perhaps withhold information for their own gain. Some bosses hold back information of redundancies for the company for some time, and then when its right they let the workers know. Two points of view: more information for the worker, this can give them empowerment to look for another job or help them make a difference so that they can be considered for new roles. Or it may set the workers into panic and everyone jumps from the sinking ship too early, and therefore the business becomes less functional. If, on the other hand the full process is visible from the beginning then the workers and unions can come. to an amicable resolve to help all the parties involved. If the bosses operate from fear they may show their true colours. Again, if only most came from a place of love and trust then these conflicts inside people (heart, soul and ego) and inside their industry would be at a minimal. If only…

What we see are people that want to make a difference in their industries and want to come forward and work for the greater good but are mistrusting of their leaders in case the carpet is ripped from underneath them and they lose their jobs. If this is the case, then trust yourself and your integrity and a new and better job will come around. We don't want you to suppress the innate goodness in yourselves. Trust us and we will deliver something even better. But remember you have to ask. With the Law of attraction, remember, think about what you want in a job or situation and the thought alone will start the energy to attracting that which you have been asking for. However, remember if you keep thinking negative thoughts and bad events then the Law of Attraction will work this way too. So, wherever possible be positive and more positive things will become attracted to you. Patience is also needed.

The more you want to learn about us and Source then the more information we will send you. Either through thought, or coincidences, or certain people coming into your lives. Notice this, and ask why and how you can learn from this person and vice versa. Remember lessons are not always positive. What a person may bring you is an unpleasant experience. You can truly learn from this and how not to do things. Humans learn more by mistakes than constant successes. A businessman who has failed will learn quickly about what not to do, instead of launching without planning they leave the space to really look for any pitfalls and successes and then figure out what can be done correctly and with integrity. So the business will be a success. Negativity attracts more negativity and positivity attracts more positivity. This is the Law of Attraction. Be mindful of your thoughts; be mindful of your actions. All are energy and we and the universe feel all of this in an energetic way. We do not judge so the Law of Attraction works both ways, we are not here to question your choices.

And so it is…

16.

Love and Differences by Mother Mary

We want to talk to you of love; how strange and peculiar it actually is. We have stated before that there are different types of love. Sibling, parental, romantic, and friendship are the most basic ones. The most important one is for the child and the parents. Parents can make or break a child. It is your responsibility to show love to vulnerable children. At birth they are helpless and dependant on someone. If you chose to have a child and they chose you then you have a responsibility to care and nurture that being. Having a baby is scary and going into the unknown for many. In a situation where they have no control it can be very upsetting until they get the hang of it. Looking after children is one of the most important jobs of your life. Those of you who chose not to have children, very commendable, and responsible, rather than being forced into something you feel you are not cut out to do. That is really looking at yourself rather than going with peer pressure, if there was any.

For those of you who have children. These beautiful young things are totally reliant on you for everything. Especially love. They will die and wilt away if you do not give them love and the loving touch of hugs and cuddles. Children are amazing and if you look closely, they will amaze you every day. Some are wise beyond their years. These are old souls. They will be more relaxed and chilled, don't get upset too easily and can cope with change. Younger souls will be more restless and inquiring. Learning what they can when they can. Every child also learns differently, and teachers are aware of this and adjust accordingly.

There are reasons why some children get sick and die early in their lives. They may have changed their mind and realised that there is more to do elsewhere. Their contract may have been only short anyway, and part of that contract is to work with the families that have to learn the lessons of grief and gratitude. Hard indeed, but some can only learn through really difficult lessons. The children of cancer are often messengers and they are very selflessly able to carry that message to the right people. When you interact with these children, they are often wise beyond their years and understand all that is. Again, another lesson for the parents. The souls are very special who opt to do this and they feel very little pain but are resigned and calm. They are often the younger sibling who want to learn quickly and work more with people. In their previous life they learnt a very stern and important lesson so that they may sacrifice themselves after such a short time on this earth.

Babies that die of natural causes have chosen this. Souls chose the parents and if there was a genetic fault, it is so people learn from this; a huge self-sacrifice for the greater good. This is how we exist here, always for the greater good, the love and peaceful solution.

By the time children start to become adults they start to notice feelings in the body and gut, they start to learn the signs of choices which are right for them or not. Getting into a car that you know isn't safe and you don't have a good feeling about it but the friends get you in the car anyway. Then something goes badly wrong.

Trust your gut. Teenagers begin to learn it there, unless they are too hedonistic or ego-driven in which case they might leave their path in an accident and have to start all over again. Young adults start to learn more too. Sometimes they think they are mistaken, no they are not. Look at the signs and signals. Look at what your teacher and master is trying to tell you. If you are connected more with spirit — what are we trying to tell you — your loved ones, your guides?

Young teenage love is very exploratory and fun. But be safe, there are still horrible people out there who have strayed off their contract and are following the ego. Be cautious and safe with the love of your friends who watch out for you. Trust and respect each other and you and your friends will have each other's backs.

Going into your 20s provide more fun times and more lessons to learn about romantic love, relationships learning the pros and cons of being in a new relationship; the hurts and the highs, enjoy and sit in all feelings, cherish the good, pause briefly in the bad and learn from them all.

By the time you get to the late 20s/early 30s then children may be on their way or in a relationship with no children, either are fine. If you cannot have children then please think of adoption and helping many of those children that deserve better; To be brought up in another loving household. The circumstances were written into the contract to come to other parents to bring them joy as the mother has had special circumstances overcome her. Perhaps a lesson in her contract is to share her baby.

It's beautiful in some collective cultures, including indigenous people, (two thirds of the worlds cultures are of a collective society in nature) how you all share the upbringing of the clan, family, extended family; this is loving and living in the ideal. However, there are some that have turned against you and do not always have the respect for all; the ego steps in and can damage others (abuse, violence or emotional trauma). Be cautious, those of you with extra senses, please keep it turned on. If you suspect someone is not acting in a loving respectful way, and yes always tell the truth even if you are threatened, we will protect you. It will work out in the end. We have to protect the vulnerable from egotistical adults that are following human ego, pleasure and causing harm to others, child rape, beatings and persecution to the young ones. Stop it where you can.

We understand and see that child pornography goes on. It saddens us as this is not in any contracts. The enablers of this will still have to come to the same place to heal and learn lessons just like everyone else. Sadly, there are some people without conscience or regret and have ego ruling to the very end. There is no judgement as we gave you choice and free will, however you are right to hold them in incarceration, to protect the innocent. They will have a shock when they get back to Source to organise their next life if they do not start suffering as they have caused in the remainder of this life.

We don't care about sex habits of whatever invention but we do care and note down if people go out deliberately to hurt others, the young, incapacitated or infirm. Or even without consent. Both parties must give consent and no hurt or injurious act unless agreed upon should happen.

Love; 'ain't it grand' only if you treat it and others with the upmost respect.

We will always love you no matter what you do or don't do (free choice, free will) and we will guide you to the next appropriate step.

And so it is…

17.

Relationships
by Quan Yin

We want to talk to you about relationships. All human dynamics can be interesting and often entertains us here. Relationships can occur through several lifetimes. The soul families can be quite large; up to about 25–30 souls together. These souls come together in their lives either in families or close-knit neighbourhoods. Or even colleagues may have worked together in other professions or in other companies. You will feel drawn to each other and get on well in the workplace. Many even form allies with you. What you will notice is that you will meet in the canteen or in meetings and there will be a feeling of being drawn towards each other. You may not understand why but you may have similar outlooks as each other. The more you feel drawn, the more lives you have spent together. Soul families may even be drawn together, which could be through marriage or business partnerships. It will be easy to get along and things will flow. There will be a pull inside that perhaps you don't understand but feel the compunction to investigate the dynamics.

Families can be drawn together through marriage as well, and it doesn't matter which gender as it is only about the soul's journey not about gender. It is about how far you are through your lives, how far you have come and how you are learning your lessons to be a better person. To help more and to assist those who are lesser in either socio-economic areas, disabilities or are ill. If you are drawn to these others then perhaps it is to help and offer unbiased or unconditional love and understanding. Often people with disabilities can see things that able-bodied people can't. Because their normal senses are compromised so the other senses pick up more from the energy of people, much like children before they have been socialised or negated in what they see.

Dynamics of parents and children in the immediate family will have lived together several times over, and are destined to continue their lives together. The dynamics are also changed in order for you to experience all forms of relationships. Parent and child, siblings, cousins can become siblings in a sequential life and parents can become children to their children. So the dynamics swap and change to work out the lessons that need to be learnt. Children who meet in schools that make lifelong friendships will have met before and lived alongside each other. They may have been to war together, or shared a situation that was life threatening or extreme. These factors often bring these souls together to share another time.

Up in Source these souls hang out together. They seem to gravitate towards each other, in Source and on Earth. With extreme feelings and adrenalin flowing, these heightened states bring people together towards a common goal. Fighting for freedom, demonstrating on the streets of a city, or going into jail and fighting for survival and a place in the pecking order. Alliances are made and are often kept due to the extreme conditions that they came together under.

Relationships between people can move and change like a body of water. They can flow without any conflict — like a river or lake, where things are as they should be. However, like a river the water eventually flows out through the exit and then the river may get a little turbulent. Again, much like relationships. Very few dynamic relationships are all smooth sailing.

This is about lessons and maturity as a soul learns how to deal with speed bumps or rocks in the rivers' path. Every meeting between two people always has a reason. Could be good or bad but as long as you learn from it, it is unlikely to come back and repeat. So, what we are saying here is that you should be aware, and travel through life with your eyes wide open and notice things. Be observant and act accordingly. 'What does this new meeting feel like? Why and what do I have to learn from this?' Every meeting has its reasons and it is up to you and your soul to feel out what this is.

You may meet someone in the street briefly — perhaps to give directions or help them on their way, or even being accosted — there are always reasons.

If this happens — being accosted, was it a pay back from karma, have you been particularly horrible to someone and ripped them off? Look hard and remember. You may be affronted by the assault and yes, it is scary. Ask yourself why did this happen? What can you see, if anyting to learn? It could be to find compassion for others. To feel how it is for those who are less fortunate and are often bullied. Were you a bully back at school? Also, karma has no notion of time and this event can come back and remind you of the learning journey that you are on. Or it could be that the assaulter has strayed off their path and you are in the wrong place at the wrong time. However, look on it as a learning moment to be able to see and feel true compassion for yourself and others. Was it meant for you or not? Only you and your soul will know.

If it is a meeting of like-minded people then there is a learning for both of you to help the community or wherever you are; office, orchard, farm, factories. All apply; it doesn't matter where it is. If you get held up on the street to give someone directions, then help as there is a reason they stopped you to ask. Help them as best you can. The reason may not be apparent to you at first but later it may. We may be setting you up for another meeting with them in that life or the next. It may have just been a preliminarily meeting to set the foundations of what will happen in the future. You just don't know. However, those of you who are through a lot of their lives will begin to realise this of meetings and random people. There is a reason, trust us.

As regards to marriage, the dynamics are very interesting and watching how they play out is often unique. Many now are coming to divorce or are splitting up even if there are children involved. This is okay too. We do not want you to be in a partnership where it does not serve you anymore. Souls come together to experience. Remember not to stick to the society's rules and values regarding marriage if it doesn't suit you and is making you sick. Don't misinterpret this as 'Ahh it's too hard and give up after a short period of time.' Relationships are work. The more mature the soul in you, the quicker you will realise this and work with the soul and heart to get the best out of it. However, if after a prolonged period of time it is still making you sick, act accordingly and deal with the hard truth. Life is full of truths and unfortunately the ego doesn't like the hard truths. It likes the easy gain, the easy life even though it will often end up harder in the long run. To be able to speak your truth is a skill in itself. It takes guts and maturity to do so. We are also talking of the maturity of the souls. Younger souls are more led by the ego and that is a lesson that they need to learn as they go through the lives. As we said before, once completed we will then discuss with the soul what it learnt and what is next to learn.

Some are destined to stay together for life, that is very admirable especially when the souls are dying. However, we don't like to see your soul wilting away. If you chose to be with that person for the good of the children, then do it with all your heart and unconditionally. However, if you feel you have worked at it, tried counselling, and other remedies and your soul is still sad then walk away amicably. It is better for the children not to be in the unhappy environment as they will pick up on the energy that is around the house. The underlying displeasure in each other will gradually grow, this is the law of attraction, the energy affects the children. Often if the spilt is amicable then the children will understand this and work through their own emotions and have a good relationship with both parents. As the children grow and mature, they can then see the truth and realise that it wasn't anything about them but more about the dynamics of the parents. (Children often take it on board themselves, if you are going through this please let your children know it is not them). It is just you (parents) who are working out a lesson with your soul and things will eventually be good. The experience of this will also help others that may be going through it. Or later in life you come across a similar predicament and you can help and support your friend that may be going through this. Remember these experiences were sent because you chose them, and the lessons are imperative in order to help others either in this life or the next, or the next... depending on the contract.

Romantic relationships are entertaining to watch, especially those who are new to life's journey and a new soul. There always seems to such a dance when dating or getting to know someone that you have a romantic interest in.. A game of half-truths, a game of not admitting anything before the other, a game of interpretive dance in order to tell the other in a cryptic way. This is funny as you may not be on the same wavelength as each other; one may do ballet and the other rock n' roll. One must take the lead and both must speak their truth. This is difficult at times, through fear of being dumped or chastised. This is where being strong and knowing who you are is paramount. However, there is fine line of arrogance and complacency here and too much will push the other away. That is often why as young people you experience and experiment with others to find the right combination — to find the right person. And as ever there is always free will.

Trust is also earned in a relationship, often people give it too quickly. If this is the case then be prepared to be hurt. This is a lesson you have requested to learn. Let's hope you learn it quickly, or you will continue the same lesson. Be aware of what has happened and the trust that was broken. Don't take it to heart, notice how you feel and take responsibility for your actions. You are not responsible for anybody else's feelings. This is also true for other dynamics, you are not responsible for others' emotions and feelings.

What we hear is 'You made me feel this way... you make me feel like shit... you make me sad... you make me happy...' Actually, they don't — they may have been a factor in this event but you are responsible for yourselves. You can choose to be sad, jealous, angry, happy or whatever emotion has come up. Ultimately, you are responsible. You have to work through why you feel like this. Notice what comes up, why it comes up. That is often the problem that we see. That humankind is not responsible for their actions. Really? Really? We gave you free will. You choose your emotions; you choose the line of action. So many of you blame others; in the workplace, in families. It's about being aware of those that come up, the emotions, the actions and reactions. We hear it a lot, especially in the workplace, people aren't frank with each other. If everyone spoke their truth as they see it then more open discussions could occur and the real truths and reasons could be explored in a gentle, non-aggressive manner. At the moment this is only really happening with the older souls. The older souls that have been around a while, have been observing and learning their lessons. That is why they are old souls.

Relationships are dynamic and can flow and ebb. If the partnership is unequal then the weaker of the two can lose themselves and this is not ideal. It can happen if the weaker is smitten and doesn't want to do anything to jeopardise it. They will lose themselves and the stronger may not appreciate always being right or does not get a stimulating relationship where there are challenges. We see this often, it doesn't work in the long-term but instead is a really valuable lesson for them and they can correct and try again but this time with experience of a relationship that didn't work.

There is no set rule that every marriage/partnership will work for life. This is not always the soul's journey. The soul's journey is to experience as much as possible. If it can be done in one or two relationships then that is how it is written. Please don't feel bad if it doesn't work. As long as you were true to your soul and heart then you are following your contract. It is social values from over hundreds of years ago that bring on the guilt of a failed marriage. These social values are made only by one or two people, yet how can a decision like this be made for the whole country, or the followers (religion). Everyone is on a different path, a different lesson and a different level of soul journey. All powers build on guilt, all of them, especially if the union, marriage breaks down. Staying in an unhealthy relationship can make the soul sick.

We like the phrase "if you can't love the one you want then love the one you are with." This phrase promotes love; we like this. What we notice as well is with Social Media, society is put under pressure to perform; in looks, in bed, in social circles, in keeping up with your neighbours. All this choice makes people unhappy. These empty decisions about insignificant things make you unhappy because it is not what you truly want but more what you think others want of you. Your make-up has to be so, the car you buy has to be this one, and the peer pressure of accumulating things puts stress on to you; to want to fit in. If you stop trying so hard, and relax people will admire you for speaking your truth. Those who are shallow, and who you do not get on with will gradually fade away, will not vibrate at the same resonance as yourself. They will drop away as you mature and learn your lessons. Law of Attraction. Attraction to the same kind of people. You may start to feel lonely at first as the others fade away, but use this time to nurture yourself and build your skills. The vibrations will start to change like your friends.

It is just another chapter that you will go through. What will happen then is that you will start to make friends who vibrate at the same level. You will feel different and have different kind of conversations with those new people. Join a group that interests you, full of like-minded people. People you can learn from, people you enjoy laughing with. Souls change and mature as they go through life and this is very normal that groups of friends change. If this doesn't happen then the lesson is still being learnt.

In every relationship it is hard to speak your truth, and we never said it would be easy. Being true to your soul takes practice and listening skills. To be able to speak your truth in a personal relationship takes trust and understanding between the both of you. Approaching serious conversations about something you may not agree with takes maturity and honesty. If the partner is right for you then they will listen with understanding, a mind without prejudice, thoughts without chastisement. Instead they will listen with integrity and honesty and together you can sort out what is troubling the other. These times can come from fear. (F — false, E — evidence, A — appears R-real.) You do not know what the other is thinking or feeling and would be incredibly arrogant of you to think that you know. Don't underestimate your partner, give them credit and see what is going on. If you feel they are hiding something from you then ask. Feel their answer. What do you notice? What do you feel in your gut? Just mentioning this may give them a clue that you need to talk. Or that they need to rectify what is going on and talk to you about it. People hide many different things from others; affairs, gifts, surprise holidays. Remember, things are never what they seem and withholding information could be for something completely different than what you expect. Go back to F E A R, what does it mean? Unfortunately, the powers that be like the people to stay in fear. It's easier for them to control. Be it a dictatorship, a religion or what seems to be a democracy, it filters down through the hierarchy and eventually comes to the masses. Those with cleverly chosen words on television or on social media ensure the masses (young souls) are easy to control. Free thinkers in certain countries are put to death, their governments are built on fear and control their population. Keeping a lid on the workers: very clever. As we have said the powers of this kind will eventually be toppled or die and the new older souls of your generations to come will lead a better and healthier regime.

The overall message is trust yourself, your heart, and your soul. Stay and hang out with likeminded people, stay out of fear as much as possible. Be true to yourself when in a relationship and things will be as they are written in your contracts. It takes a lot of courage to be who you truly are, as well as it takes a while to find out who you truly are. Once there, be good to yourself and to others that you love.

We love you and so it is…

18.

The Arts
by Arnoah

We want you to know about music and art and how it is incredibly influential on your moods and disposition. Through art you can express yourself in another dimension. In another medium. Art has been used for many things; helping children get over trauma, and to help mentally ill people express themselves. It has helped inmates in the prison system to cope with the time inside. Art and painting can be used whilst meditating to help express what you see in the other world, the other dimensions. Some clairvoyants use art as an expressive tool of spirituality. Some can use this medium to help give you messages about how or what may be going on. The clairvoyants and mediums produce beautiful work and so individual to express your life and personality as well as your contract. Using charcoals or pastels to draw a picture as it comes to them. Art comes in many different mediums including, sculpting, papier-mâché, bronze, carved limestone. The tools of the artist of painting also come in many different media including pastels, charcoal, oils, acrylics. Find your medium. If you have a propensity towards the arts then explore. Perhaps this is the way that you can help people with their outcomes.

As you branch into clairvoyance the drawings and paintings may be the way that sits well with you and can help others. You don't have to be a practiced artist; you just have to start practicing. You only have to pick up an implement and start.

If you look around at the great pieces of art in the world what do they evoke in you? How do they make you feel? The Sistine Chapel and the Michelangelo painting of God and Adam? Then there is the Mona Lisa, what does that mean to you and how does it feel when you look at that kind of art? There are many different types of styles and mediums in art. So many great artists; Miro, Picasso, Monet, Dali. So many styles to choose from; Abstract, realism, romanticism-

How do the strokes of the brush, pastel, charcoal, or pencil feel on the page to you? Do you feel comfortable or awkward? Think of someone — a friend, relative ask their permission to do something for them. Find the nothingness and feel what comes up. Direct your focus to them, and paint. See what comes up, maybe there are messages that need to come through. Link and sync into their space and watch what appears beneath your hand. Remember anything is possible and there are no hard and fast rules. No restrictions, if there are any you have made them up in your own mind and societal influence has found a way in. Stop it. You cannot hurt anyone so let the guides and spirits take over your hand, relax and watch what comes out. If you practice then it will become second nature like any other clairvoyant practice.

Music is a mathematical language but in the right hands it can say so much, with so much expression and take the listener to another place completely. If you are already a musician, great, and if not pick an instrument. You will have felt drawn to music if this is your talent and contract. You will have perhaps tried many different instruments and found your favourite. Once you get proficient at it, and this is dedication then you can lose yourself in the crotchets and minims. If you don't read music that is great also. It often means as well that you are not so restricted to what someone else has written. Then the boundaries fall away and the music sings out into the ether.

Music, like drawing has come from the very beginning of time when humans first started to bang sticks and drums together. Music evokes spirits too. Given the right tone and rhythm, so ceremonies of ancients took place. The Native Americans have been doing this as far as they can remember. Their spirit Gods and ancient medicine men signalled to each other and communicated for the greater good. With music and ceremonies, cultures around the world speak to us. We love the beats, and the sounds that humans have learnt to evoke from instruments. There are many clever musicians that make their instruments sing. It is beautiful to hear our Angels sing too and it sounds divine, and this evokes higher vibrations when listened to. They often sing over here and we — the masters, teachers, loved ones and other spirit guides all gather to listen.

It is tranquil and enjoyable. Sometimes past great artists also join in. The making of music and sounds makes us happier, if that is even possible. We enjoy so much and when a great musician comes to pass over after the repair of the soul with the body of injury or disease, we are very enthused to hear them play. It is a wondrous moment.

Different beats and rhythms can change a vibration of someone, can raise it or bring it down. Your brains and bodies resonate at different levels. When we say raise your vibrations, music can certainly help. Certain tones can help you heal and repair. Other tones help get rid of unwanted thoughts, guilt or sadness, and other tones open your chakras in order to get to a higher vibration in meditation. Your bodies vibrate and move constantly, certain tones enhance that. Even voice spoken or singing can change the vibration. The constant hum in your body if you are singing will change the molecules. That is why when monks Buddhists, Hindus, Catholics are learning to meditate at a higher level to get them closer to Source they chant. Gregorian monks chanted many years ago, Catholic priests and clergy pray out loud and this raises the vibration, Hindu priests chant OM and this one universal sound raises their vibration to get to the next level of meditation. They chant for hours and this makes the whole-body sing on a level that is not normal for Westerners. The training can be quite intense and is a discipline. In the Islamic faith praying to Mecca five times a day raises the vibrations as well.

Some wise gurus — Hindus and Buddhists that travel the world spreading the word have concerts and play instruments to evoke the opening of the chakras. They sound incomplete on their own but with other overlay of melodies they are very easy to listen to. These sounds awaken the energy centres in your body. Feel how this is. Notice what you feel in each centre. Don't be afraid to open the chakras, by being open you are also open to receive downloads from us to help your DNA to settle and change to be more open to receiving messages. You cannot hurt yourself with your chakras open. If you are learning now, then make sure that you ask the four directions to protect you from entities. Trust us, trust yourself, trust the process. We will protect you but also please remember to ask.

Music brings people together through concerts, festivals and togetherness. People gather as a group to have a good time, for celebrations as well as funerals. All major events have music, even the streets with buskers bring people together. People are happy dancing and singing. . All major events have music. People listen with headsets, in the car and in the workplace. We believe more music should be piped into offices to help them keep calm. Perhaps some of the chakra tones or Alpha, Beta, or Gamma will help concentration. These tones are so low that most people will be unaware of it. Or have them on at home whilst the kids are doing their homework.

Both music and art are great healers for many different dispositions. It helps with rehabilitation; it helps give confidence and belief in yourself. Don't be over critical of yourself. Take it easy, relax and enjoy that way of expression, and on a level you will heal. Have music around you that evokes happiness and love. These media are even more potent when using them in your healing of others and yourself. Express in the way you feel comfortable. Practice, practice, practice.

Dance is another great way of healing, keeping fit and smiling. It has so many benefits that with both music and dance there can be amazing change. Just be aware of the changes. Notice how you feel to begin with then check in with yourself and see how you feel afterwards. Dance is linked to music so any form of this expression is awesome. We love to see people dance and have fun. Dance is also great for children in that they can experiment with their bodies and how far they can reach, jump and bound with dance. It shows their nervous systems where they are in this space. It helps their development in their minds and their bodies, to form a link of good communication between the two parts as you are all a whole. Dance with your children, play music with your children have fun; they are your future.

We love you and express yourself.

19.

Religion
by Arnoah

We want to talk to you about religion. For the most part religion has helped a lot of people. However, it is a shame that is often ruled and ordered to keep control of the populous. For a good part religion gives people a sense of belonging; it gives them a sense of purpose. It helps people look at themselves mostly and see how they can help people who are not as able as others.

For the most part it is a wonderful thing to give people strength and hope for the next part of their lives. It can help get people out of addiction, to give them a welcome when all those relatives or friends have turned against them due to their bad behaviour. It gives them a second chance as everyone deserves a second chance, if not more. Sometimes, these people who have strayed off the path of their contract have other things going on. There are several different elements that push the soul off the path. Addiction is something that most people have to learn to cope with at some stage in their life journey. A little compassion to these people will go a long way. Sympathy and helpfulness aids these people to find their way.

There are also entities from the darker side that can latch on to people if they are unaware of their presence. These little entities are a bit like bad fairies in that they can influence your thoughts and processes that you use throughout the day. Sometimes these energy balls or entities can hang around areas where misfortunes have taken place. For example, if you have been to an area where some have committed suicide then the souls are likely to hang around these areas. The Golden Gate Bridge, San Francisco is one of them, as there have been many suicides from the bridge. Other places like canyons, or hotel rooms where this happened or areas where there have been unfortunate events like rape and muggings in dark bush areas, alleyways; all leave entities around. If a person who is ignorant and open may pick up these things. Also, people with dark powers can inflict these entities onto people that they have a design on to make their life miserable. And they can. They can bring misfortune to the family; they can give you unhappy, unpleasant thoughts. So much so that you think these thoughts are actually formed in your own head and are your own terrible thoughts. They are not. They can influence your thought pattern into thinking you are depressed and sad for perhaps for no reason at all. One day you were feeling fine then something latches on to you and you start a downward spiral. Where are these thoughts coming from you wonder? Gradually you will keep bringing yourself down until you think you need medication or peer pressure to visit the doctor to have medication prescribed. Please seek out other professionals even if you think they are kooky or weird. Some would refer to these as Energy healers, Spiritualists, Shaman, Tohunga (Maori). Sometimes these alternatives are worth exploring. What happens is that they latch on to you. You may feel tingles at first but shake them off, for not knowing what they are or think you are cold and you get goose-bumps. Seers will notice that a dark patch around your aura is poisoning it. The dark entities can influence your thought process. If this is not your norm then something needs to be done. Certain practitioners — energy healers, will help and engage with the auric field and dispel the entity. Depending on how strong they are may then take a couple of tries. When the entity realises that you want it to leave, they can hold on tightly. Do not engage in niceties as they don't care, they just want your soul. Seers can engage with them then tell them in no uncertain terms to leave. With a strong persona and skills, this will happen. Once this process is completed you will feel lighter and more at ease. It may take several days to percolate through, and gradually your thought patterns will lift and get lighter. More happy thoughts will come in and your processes will be more positive.

    We are sorry that there are these things but as with everything there are opposites — good/bad, dark/light, yin/yang and many more. These little energy balls have not come back to Source but instead feel that they want others to pay for their misfortune. They want payback or so they believe. However, they haven't figured out that they actually have to do some work as well, just like we all do. Often, they will be past suicides or murder victims that haven't been able to crossover to us in Source. After a while they forget and instead get hooked into the sadness and badness of life and this then fuels them to continue.

Some churches and other religions can help be rid of these entities through love and compassion. Gradually the goodness of the congregation will help dispel them, but without knowing what is actually happening.

For the most part organised religion is a wonderful thing. It still sends the message of goodness, compassion and love. These are essential for human growth spiritually. It is unfortunate that some at the head of the different religions are driven by their egos and selfishness to grow their fortune instead. We see certain religious leaders taking advantage of the congregation by taking their money and donations and using it for their own gain. Some went into the church (Christianity and Catholicism) for job security and gain, not for the true reasons of what the church originally stood for.

All religions are the same with greedy people at the top. As with governments this will gradually change as the people change. It will take generations but it will happen. It is happening now with the current Pope Francis and he is making change for the greater good.

We understand why they do this but we don't like the fact that some leaders take advantage of the children, the leaders are supposed to come from a place of implicit trust yet take advantage of the young ones. When they arrive at Source, they will have lessons to learn This doesn't just happen in religions we might add but also in institutions that look after children. All are wrong. This is not in their contracts, the persecutors or the children. The offenders have strayed off their contract and can be influenced by entities but have been in this state of mind for quite some time and have now taken advantage of weaker people.

Some religions distort the truth from God for their own gain and the gain of that religion. Many of the religions have taken things out of context, to enable the followers to worship the way the leaders have decreed . The few Muslims and we mean a very few have taken Jihad ("effort" struggle on behalf of God and Islam —*Oxford language dictionary*.) to the extreme, struggle against opposing enemy, in order to maim or kill. Most are peaceful people and do not agree what the others are doing — most believe Jihad is a struggle against sin and temptation, much like Lent — Catholicism/Christianity. We feel that a particular sect of the Islamic faith is going too far. They are not allowing other religions and groups to worship the way they want to. The Muslim minority have taken things out of context. As we mentioned before this faith is based on violence and suppression. The other faiths are from love and compassion. including Catholicism, Christianity, Hinduism and Sikhism. All speak of a way of defence of their doctrine through whatever means necessary, but this is only the last resort.

Spirituality is a faith but not an ordinary faith. There is no head of the organisation. We allow people to come across spirituality on their own inquiries. We do not force it on you. There is no ceremony to bring you into to the church. There is no church; there are only your beliefs, what you have started to notice as regards what you see beyond normality. The surrounding energies circulates for you to sense or feel, including loved ones and spirit guides. We want no money, there is no hard and fast rule when you should worship. You can pray and talk to us at any time in any place. Jesus, Yogananda, Mary, St Francis, St Germaine, (French Saint protector of abused children), Mohammed, Buddha, Osho and many others that you know, are all here with us.

We want you to be happy. We want you to learn. We want you to show compassion. Essentially these are the traits of all religions but it is unfortunate that certain religions have begun to brainwash for their own accumulation of wealth. What we see are many unselfish people go into the religion and want to help others — this is very commendable but unfortunately, they may get corrupted by the time they start to move up the ladder. The preaching of the holy books, have begun to get distorted for the good of the higher rulers, priests, clergys, brahmans, alims, allamaha and almami (West African Muslims) . Essentially all these religious texts are from the truth but what the teachings have become is the controller of the people. The teachings do not allow acceptance of other faiths. There are only a certain few fundamentalists, that take the gospel as the final word. Not allowing other possibilities to occur. All things and inventions come from us and the foresight of the bigger picture. The rules and regulations we feel are a little constrictive. Some religion factions do not allow spirit to come through and believe that these people who are seers are mad or are blasphemers. They don't allow homoeopathy to be used, also believe that Tarot is from the devil (to us it's just another way of communicating). They don't let people who love the same gender as themselves into the some of the religious factions. It is referred to in the Vatican. (*Referred to "intrinsically disordered and contrary to natural law" Catechism Nos: 2357-59*). These smaller sects are becoming less in numbers and becoming more understanding. There is also persecution of homosexuals in many Arab states (Saudi Arabia follows the Sharia law forbidding same sex relationships punishable by death) and it is mentioned in the Koran. There is now a new movement coming through with a different interpretation which is more accepting. As we said before all souls are equal it is just their skill set and knowledge that can be at a different level. The souls of people who are homosexual are equal to any other soul too and should not be persecuted or imprisoned as they are just being true to who they really are. Remember lives are about experiences and many if not all will sample a life in this way.

Life is about acceptance and forgiveness. Treating people as you would expect to be treated. Treat all others with respect, non-judgement and equally.

Unfortunately, some religions indoctrinate younger people to help them fight their war in the name of God. WE DO NOT WANT WAR. There are always other ways to find a peaceful solution and both parties have to want to do this. There has to be compromise. Do not kill in the name of God. Don't use us as an excuse to kill people. It is for the gain of the top rulers, be it in corporations and munitions selling or the leaders of the country, to grow their own personal wealth. We don't want this. It is unnecessary and no good can come of war.

We want you all to get on with each other, no one religion is better than the other. As long as an organised religion offers solace, help, compassion and love we couldn't ask for anything else. If you don't feel comfortable about what is being taught then ask about the lesson. Feel if it sits right with you and your soul. What do you notice when the congregation come together? Is there happiness, elation? Does it make you feel awkward or uncomfortable? Feel the words being said — do they come from a place of genuine love? Do the vibrations of the words lift your whole being? If so then you are in the right place, if not look elsewhere. Not all will suit all, so go and look, feel other places, other religions and if nothing fits be who you are and come from a place of love.

Trust yourself, you will have done the work now trust us and other like-minded people. You will know the truth, your truth and the truth of the leaders. Be wary and trust your soul, gut and what it is telling you. Don't succumb to bullies and peer pressure, you are your own master. Live it your way.

It is as it is…

20.

Truth
by Archangel Micheal

We want to talk to you of truth. Many have the compunction not to be truthful either through fear or through habit. We want you to be your true selves. That means standing in your truth and learning how to stand up with pride in knowing who you truly are. Part of life and this contract is about finding your way in this world in order to help Gaia and the others around you.

We often find the reason people lie is for their immediate gain and hedonism. People lie to protect themselves. We are sure that if everyone spoke their truth as they see it then the world would be far more transparent. We have mentioned before about visibility but unfortunately the governments want to keep the absolute truth from you. This will not change until the powers trust the people that they will understand their reasons for making those decisions and allow the greater good to come through. Some world leaders believe this but only a special few. At the moment, the world leaders do not trust that they will not be taken down and out of their power. There needs to be trust both ways. It is unfortunate that many members of parliaments do not trust their people and so the people feel this and do not trust their governments.

Truth is hard to say as many think they will offend but if everyone used the power of acceptance and realised that the truth is more important than bad information that you think they want to hear. If you are a genuine person that stands in their truth then speaking untruths will jar your very being. It goes against everything you have worked for and will make you sick if you don't continue to be your true self. Others lie because they believe if they don't then it will not work or they won't get what they want, or they won't get their desired outcome. Just a thought, perhaps that isn't the correct outcome and that another result could be better. However, if you use the truth and all around you have candid conversations you will probably find in the long-run that the results are far superior and work better than the untruth or lies that try to get you the desired outcome. Not only that lies eventually come out and the end result will be affected. It causes greater stress and man power to recorrect the problem that was discovered. Finding out that it was based on lies and misinformation. Lying in the work place is so counterproductive that others around you will begin to mistrust you and will never feel comfortable in doing business with you. It is not necessary. The truth always comes out and then a repair has to happen for the hurt and used people as well as for yourself as you have to re-adjust your thinking, planning and back tracking on your story. If you don't then you may have to find another job. Is it really worth it? We think not. We feel not.

Personal relationships based on lies won't work either. All great relationships and long-lasting relationships are built on truth and compassion. If you lie to your loved one and they find out will they ever trust you again? If you have a dark secret that you think they won't accept then is the relationship really worth it? If they cannot love and accept you for who you are then is this the relationship you want to spend a lot of time in? How would the guilt feel if you kept on having to hide, or they may talk to the wrong person and something slips out? Mistrust starts to fester and grow. The partner may never trust you again, unless they are truly evolved and then they can feel how it is. Even then, you may not be saved in your untruths.

The relationship with your children should also be built on trust. Acceptance that your children have their own personalities, that they are growing and exploring in this world and finding their way. Instil in your children that if they tell the truth there will be very little or no punishments then they are more likely to come clean. If they break a vase or something that might be precious to you then if they admit immediately that they broke it, and then dealing with the outcome in a gentle way, in an accepting way; "oops accidents happen — let's clean up the mess." This way builds confidence that if they do something wrong, they can come and tell you about it. Often children see programs on television that shows parents exploding at a misdemeanour and this gives the wrong impression for your children and they think you will react that way. Please put them straight and through experience you will realise that you have got a really good relationship with your children. It begins in the beginning from a very early age. They learn early and will grow up with more trust and being given the strength to speak their truth. Your reaction as parents is so important in the beginning so that once they grow older the element of trust is there between you.

Once they are teens they may start experimenting. They find alcohol, sex, drugs and all the other attractive things that teenagers want to find out about. It is nature and their huge desire to learn what is out there in the world. The parents have sheltered them until high school and then other personalities come in to the forefront and all are finding their way and how to interact with different people. Remember the Law of Attraction means friends will gravitate towards each other. If you feel your child is being influenced by another that you do not feel is healthy then have a chat with your teenager. Find out about them; listen without prejudice and no judgement. If you listen with an open mind, then you can gather all the information and act accordingly. Ask them questions… Why do you like that friend? How do they serve you? What do you like about hanging with them? Why do you do alcohol and drugs? What does it do for you? Open a conversation with them and find out why they do these things. We know that drugs in most countries are illegal and so is underage drinking but most kids will try and do them both. It's about exploring and sampling all that is available. Do you remember being a kid, or teenager? Recall how it was for you. There is even more stress now for teenagers to perform in the best possible way. Social media judges on looks, judges on accomplishments good and bad. The pressure to perform in both academic and leisure time is extraordinary. It is pushing them to try extremes, to better the next prank. All you can do as parents is have their backs, trust them and allow them to experiment in a safe area. If that means drinking or smoking, then is it better to have their trust rather than the teenagers going to a place where they will get arrested and then you have to deal with the outcome.

Talk to your children about truth and lies. Explain that truth will always win and will always come out, maybe not now but later for sure. It takes a lot of brains to lie and cheat, you have to be on alert all the time, always looking over your shoulder in case someone finds out. Much better to come clean and deal with the consequences. This way is a huge growth for your soul and helps with the learning of the lessons of your contract in order to move on and grow to the next life.

We find everybody does a little lying, and you may not even realise. Half-truths are interesting, even exaggerations are half-truths, but we get this especially if you are a storyteller. The exaggeration can make for a great story but again remember the truth will always come out eventually. It's really simple DON'T LIE… Speaking the truth is not always easy and we get that, but these are the lessons of the life that you have chosen. The truth when it comes out will benefit the long game not the short game. So, you have to trust the purpose of what you are speaking and the purpose of what you hope to accomplish. If there is good to come about, it will, but not always in the way that you expect or have planned for. As with everything when we work with you the outcome will be the best for the greater good. If you feel you have not benefitted like you thought you would then trust that the correct outcome will eventuate as it should and in the Divine Plan. If your plan is formed with integrity and purpose for the greater good then it will happen.

It will be what it will be… the truth.

21.

Sentiment and Affront by Arnoah

We want to talk to you of sentiment. It's about noticing the feelings of others and being aware of how others feel. You go through life like a pinball machine randomly bumping into others at random times. With others and their feelings sometimes, it may feel like a minefield when dealing with particularly sensitive friends or relatives. Some people take affront at anything and get defensive; from the news, a passing comment in the street, a notice on the wall. Some of these things people take umbrage from and get all hot under the collar. We find this fascinating especially the way some people plump up their feathers and start to have a feeling of importance and justification if something affronts. One of the first things you need to look at is whether the person is having a joke or is serious. What did they really mean by that comment, why did it affect you so? Remember if people are mean then you need to look at where they came from in order to say a comment like that. You do not know their past, and what they have been through. You are not judge and jury for that person on the comment that they made. This is a big part of acceptance, to let things slide and not to take things on board that do not serve you. Do not retaliate if you can stop yourself in time. Take your time, assess the situation, and pause before commenting. If you want to know the truth of that person and where they are coming from then ask them. What warranted such an interesting comment. If they have had personal experience of being mugged by an individual from a particular race or culture which has led them to have racist opinions about an entire culture, then this may help explain why. Again, remember things are not what they seem at first and there are always layers of that person that they are working through for themselves. For you to jump down their throats also speaks volumes of yourself. You have judged that person for that comment without getting the whole facts. This experience may have been written into their contract and the ego is biting back over it. Perhaps they feel that they need to be down on those people by grouping the culture together even though only one has hurt them. They also need to look at themselves to figure out why this was happening to them. If you don't retort to that derogatory comment then think about it.

If you were hurt or affronted by that comment why have you taken it on board? It's their stuff, their emotions, their anger, jealousy, frustration from past experiences coming through. This is again acceptance. Does your opinion change of them from that comment? Or are you still good friends or acquaintances and nothing between your dynamics has changed. If it has changed then you have made a judgement and have changed the level of vibration that you work with, the vibration has dropped. Love is a higher vibration as we said before, but judgement is much lower. Be mindful of your reaction and not judge the individual or the culture, you are all souls trying figure out a way through with challenges and lessons to grow and learn.

Do you want to sit in judgement and stay stagnant? Do you not want to grow, shake off the baggage you have and work through your karma to get to the next life and the next lesson? We find people as we have stated before are afraid to speak their truth. This is a perfect example, if a comment is offensive then open that discourse and find out why. Others will learn by your candour and follow your lead. We find equally evolved people, light workers, and last life souls have found a way of sitting with these comments and do not take it on board or take offence. They know that it isn't their emotions, past hurts, anger or frustration and their processes of pealing back the layers are almost complete. They are sure of who they are and have developed the strength to stand up for themselves. These people will smile to themselves and think 'ah, well, they have more lessons to learn, they will not get a rise out of me as it is not worth my time, effort and space in my head'. Rise above the comments and know that they are coming from an insecure place to say something like that. If people verbally attack you and you feel you have done nothing wrong then they are coming from a very desperate place and the ego has taken over to get great gains from you or the situation.

It is lovely that lots of you take time to spoil friends and family, to help them with birthdays and parties and to do something special for someone every so often. Kind people make an effort and go out of their way to help others and this is very commendable as long as you are not doing it for the recognition and kudos to be highly praised and a stroked ego.

No, please do it because you want to help others from the purest form of love. Humans are social creatures and need the others to feel safe and secure. It is great that there are big families that help each other, get together for celebrations and have a close-knit community. The families that are functional are normally much healthier. However, we have seen very dysfunctional families that start to cause hurt and offense within the clan. Or an elder has a particular way of doing things and the younger generation do not. We see times are changing from the old draconian way of ruling to allowing differences and personalities to come through. Now, humans can express themselves through art, fashion and colour so much more and it is wonderful to see.

We like that you remember past wars and recognise the hurt and pain that went with them. However, a quiet remembrance from all and a quiet prayer and the past soldiers recognise this and hear your prayers of thanks. It's lovely that you keep artifacts, pictures, family heirlooms as well as traditions of old (including stories and rituals) that are memorable to you and that you treasure them and then hand down to your family. Some generations will take care of those precious things and others will not and may find that they lose them in house moving and the rituals and traditions may gradually fade.

Attachment to things is interesting. If you have great sentimental value on stuff, are afraid to lose them, then there is a slight ego factor in there. Ego likes attachment to physical items. It holds you on this earth. It throws in emotion if you lose something and you start to get sucked into the emotional vortex that can be downwards spiralling. Sure, if you do lose something it is sad as it may have many memories with it, but those memories are stored in your head. They can be awakened and you can remember every day that special memory. You actually do need articles to function, clothes, kitchenware, washing facilities, transport, cars, but how much do you really need? It is worth mastering non-attachment to surplus goods. Buddhists practice nonattachment and it is hard but it is their greater belief in Source that keeps them on this path. The Western world has huge amounts of attachment to goods. Manufacturers are always pushing everyone to buy more; you need this, you want this, and you have to have that. Advertising makes you believe that you cannot live without a product. This of course is so far from the truth, unless of course the product keeps you alive, e.g. the need for electricity if you have an alarm for your health. In the Western world you will never starve, will always have clean water, and always have clothes. The choice of products can make you unhappy, always wanting more. When will you be sated? When is enough, enough? It's nice to have decent things, but you do not need 30 pairs of trousers, you do not need 100 pairs of shoes. Do you keep them for sentimental value, or do you actually use them all, certainly not all at once? If more of you bought less, the sales market would reduce, manufacturing would become less, and the Earth's supplies would be saved and not depleted.

Sentimental attachment to physical things can be a burden unless you can cope if they are lost. We are not saying, don't care about belongings but look after what you have and there will be a finite time when these things leave you. Then you must deal with the hurt and sadness that you don't have them anymore. Much like what you perceive as a hurtful comment. Look at yourself, see what you feel about the situations and things. Go within and quieten your mind, listen to your soul and heart to hear what they are saying to you. Ego and attachment go hand in hand. These things do not let you grow. It's like these things are a ball and chain around your ankle stopping you from flying high on life and to Source.

Assess how you deal with people who can rub you up the wrong way, assess what is really important to you, assess what you really need. Find the time to take stock of what is around you in your house, look at what you have. Are there other people that could benefit from the things that no longer serve you? Recycle if possible, thus lowering the output in the factories. Well, we can hope that but at the moment it's all about money making and until the world starts to change in a couple of decades then it will keep pumping out useless things.

Look at how you are with your family, what do you notice with them? How do you interact and do you take affront at something a member of the clan has said? Don't rise up, remember take a moment and chat about that comment. However, some family members won't want you to do that as it means that they have to explain themselves, they may get grumpy when asked to explain themselves, but persevere as much as you feel is necessary. These comments when asking them to explain can help them learn how it is for them and to look at themselves, or realise that actually they were spinning lies and have been caught out. Some may turn on you, be patient and stand in your power, stay calm and tranquil and they will see this in you and hopefully this will rub off on them. Again, Law of Attraction, your calm behaviour will attract more calm and worthwhile behaviour. Once the family realise that you are only after the truth or a valid explanation as to why they said these things then the discussion is on an even keel.

These skills of sentiment and listening will become easier when dealing with not so evolved beings and this is your path you have chosen, to help them, to teach them and to experience them.

Be kind and stand in your power…

Amen.

22.

Disease and Contracts by Quan Yin

We want you to know that there may be trouble afoot. The world leaders are stirring something up that ultimately will not serve mankind. We see disease becoming more prolific in the growing populations. The governments will need to help the poor and the infirm by giving them special healthcare and assistance through welfare benefits and payments. We have seen bad flus; viruses and other autoimmune diseases escalate in recent times.

The stress that people are putting themselves through to keep performing for the ego has had an impact on the body. By pushing on with your ego's desire so the body with the soul and heart have been struggling. The soul is being ignored and the ego is shouting loud to keep up with the Jones's or habits that do not serve or the true narcissism that drives the ego.

The stress that modern-day foods cause is surprising and unbelievable. What you are doing to your food is sacrilege. All the food that Gaia produces for the human body has been taken to the extreme of production. The large corporations are tampering with your food, putting in chemicals such as additives, sugars, aspartame, colourings as well as the herbicides and pesticides that stay in your food that the human body cannot metabolise. These chemicals lay dormant in the body until such time as stress takes over, the immune subsystem becomes compromised and the chemicals break down the body leading to cancer or other autoimmune diseases such as arthritis, MS, MD, Parkinson's, Motor Neuron Disease and many more. The gradual breakdown starts by feeding your children with chemical foods, this starts polluting the liver early. The sugar that is put in front of the young ones (through baking, sweets, biscuits) is starting a new habit of craving for sugar. The sweets, bars, ice-creams, burgers and many more treats are all at kids' level in the supermarket. The advertising on the television starts to corrupt at a very early age. The large fast food chains use this and get them hooked so that their sales are boosted. They are very clever in appealing to children. It is unfortunate that the parents are so stressed that it takes an iron will to say no to your child. So, the child gets their way and eats highly produced food. Some outlets try to sell good food, healthy food but unfortunately the growing of some of those foods are so contaminated by chemicals that in a micro level they are breaking down your cells to make way for new diseases.

We see you have been fighting bacteria and, in your battle, came antibiotics. We commend that and therefore more lives were saved however now with all the overuse of antibiotics there are new strains coming through and healthcare professionals have no defence. The bacteria are growing and changing. The vaccinations ultimately corrupt the young baby's DNA when the child starts to grow.

http://www.chiropractic.org/wp-content/uploads/2018/12/1200-studies-The-Truth-Will-Prevail-3.pdf *pg 76.*

We know that this is a lot of the pharmaceutical companies pushing their products to make more money. We also know that for some children this can have catastrophic results meaning the chemicals in the vaccine can affect the chemistry of the body and change the growth of that child. Not all, but some. We understand that some of these vaccines have to happen as diseases were killing masses of people all over the world. But as with everything, humans and the egos at the top get greedy. They want more money for themselves and their stakeholders. Do they not think of the little children that will suffer? What if their children became sick or disabled shortly after a vaccination how would they feel then? Again, it is much like leaders sending the army to war and them dying, the leaders don't think of themselves actually going to war and perhaps dying. It is the same for vaccinations. If you choose to vaccinate your children keep them healthy and do it after five years old. Some diseases can be beaten by good old fashion remedies. Ask your grandmother; ask your local healers who use local plants. Trust them, they know what they are doing and many blood lines have the knowledge passed down through generations. Listen to them. The other problem is that you do not give yourself time to heal. People just keep rushing, going to work sick and feel they cannot take time off due to stress in the office. Or that they feel they are letting people down if they take a couple of days off sick. The body gets sick because it is under stress and is exposed to germs. In some contracts it is written into their life about a life-threatening disease. This is to teach and show how it is to suffer a disability or a long-term disease. By going through these issues, the person can learn how it is to be on the other side of the bed. You have to rely on others and their care. How it is to feel pain, and bodily distress. We ask that you learn from these lessons. Also, to understand that sometimes you have these things written it into your contract. To go through this lesson is to teach empathy and sympathy as well as acceptance for the infirm and the sick. Just like children suffering with cancer who are here to bring families together and help them learn to come together and communicate as well as be here for a short time because they feel they are not ready for this human life and the energy is too heavy or the timing is wrong for them. To be with people who are incapacitated is for you to understand how it is for them. These extreme problems of health help you to learn acceptance as well as to signal to you to take better care of yourselves.

As we said before, eat well, and as fresh as possible, exercise and be outside smelling the flowers, feeling the sea breeze or listen to the whispers amongst the trees on a windy day. Feel the rain on your face and splash in puddles and laugh. Laughter and love will diminish disease. Acceptance of yourself leads to self-love. Many of you don't have this. Love yourself and then you can truly love another.

Love is the ultimate vibration. Live in love as much as possible and disease that you must experience will be minimal. Like the raising of your vibration through love you can also raise it through music. Together love and music will assist the feeling of higher vibration, your body will buzz and you feel so happy, elated and yet very content grounded and alive.

The food industry needs to look at their processes. Even though in the short term it will be more costly to change their practices to the 1940's and 1950's before chemicals came in to general circulation. The changeover may take some time but it will benefit all ultimately in the future. Keeping your food practices clean and chemical free is great. We see there are people who have made pesticides out of natural products. We see that some farmers are using the gentler machinery, or manual labour in harvesting, to stop the damage of the crop and preventing so much go to waste that the machines may not pick up. We see that the cultivation of herbs is growing as are organics. It makes us unhappy to see that the corporates are still pouring chemicals and rubbish into food. Even plastic made to look like rice then feeding it to the poor to make them feel full instead of giving them pure rice. No wonder people are getting sicker. It is not only diseases of the body that are brought on by bad food practices but also these chemicals can affect the mind too. Heavy metals that are in your food are also dumped in your body and your brain. These weaknesses get passed down to your children and thus compromises their immune system. Then they get vaccinated after six weeks and that will have an effect on the system. Some children are very sensitive, especially those of the new order of Goddesses and Warriors who have come to save the world as the new generation. Now the food and the chemicals are hurting them, weakening them and making it more of a challenge to get up and stop the ego system of the governments. It is almost as if elites of society who want to keep the world for themselves are starting on the innocent with their long-term plan in keeping the strong, weak, so they therefore cannot fight back. However, it is not all doom and gloom.

We are noticing that more people are buying organic, and are standing up to some of those food processes that are around in the factories. We notice more and more people exposing the bad food practices on social media and making more people aware of what is going on. But the system is keeping the majority busy, stressed and sick so weakening their defences. The small investigators or conspiracy sleuths put unfavourable reports on social media, if against any of the large companies then the articles are squashed and lost in the circus, stopping any traction to get up and running. But the good news is that more and more people are managing to share these stories and eventually the masses that complain will get too big for the companies to supress it any more.

The next generations are the ones to learn from the adults; how to demonstrate, to make truths known and expose the bad guys.

Don't give up hope, ask us to help you on your journey of food and chemicals to expose the companies that are not ethically sound. Again, you have to ask and we will send more help. And if more ask more often, then this will gain traction and energy to make something happen that no one will be able to understand. It could be a natural disaster around the manufacturing areas of chemicals. It may just be unexplainable. For others who are exposing the truth, ask for protection and we will protect you. If you have to go to court for demonstrating or are arrested due to those practices or are a journalist and need our help, just ask please and we will be there right behind you. See if you can feel us there or even catch a glimpse of one of us. Or maybe the lights will flicker or it will grow weirdly cold. We will be there.

Look after your food, look after your medicinal herbs and your healers, and look after your activists. There will be a change.

We love Gaia, we love you…

23.

Learning and Practice by Quan Yin and Archangel Micheal

There are many of us here in Source and we are here to help you. In times of trouble and times of elation. We are here for you. All that has to happen is that you are able to connect with us and hear us through practice of these skills.

We want you to be aware of how you start to feel. How the master and teacher communicate with you. Generally, it is the same for most but there are always subtle differences to each person and how they translate sensations and messages.

Often the loved ones in your family hang around those who still need their comfort if they have recently passed. Once the loved ones are repaired; when the person passes, the energy of that body must become whole, the soul is all part of this. The energy of the tissue, cells and the energy of the soul or heart must become whole again. Then they will come and assist you in your life. If you do not believe, then that is okay too. The loved ones will help and be there for the partners who are still around and managing to get through life. It takes a long time for people to get over their loved ones, especially if they have no belief system. The loved ones are often watching from afar until such time when they start to believe or when in pain or sadness, they start to call out their name. Grief is a hard emotion to bear. Instead of dwelling on the sad times, the feeling that you miss them and wish they were here to share that moment, try asking them to come to you and be there with you. If you don't believe, just ask anyway and hedge your bets. The non-believers can't prove that we don't exist over here at Source, but they also can't prove that we do. What we shall do with the non-believers is start making things happen that cannot be explained scientifically. The lights will flicker as we have mentioned before or things may move around the house. They will think they left things in one place but finds them in another place completely. These little things will help the one who is grieving. Even though at first, they may think someone is playing a cruel trick; we are not. We come from a place of love and the passed loved one is only coming from truth and love too. If you have fellow friends and family that who are non-believers, if they are okay to approach then ask them if they have noticed anything strange or unusual. Sometimes it can be a smell that they are very familiar with, this will often jolt them as smell is a very powerful reminder of that person.

Loved ones also connect using dream states but unfortunately people think it was just a dream as they miss them so much. If this is the case, then the loved ones will keep coming back and remind them of their lives in dreams. They may also need to receive important messages regarding their lives and paths. All we can do is keep trying through love to help them see what else is out there. It isn't just bricks, mortar and organics; it is also energy, resonance, heat or cool, shivers, goose bumps, unusual sensations about the body and feelings of magnetic pulls to certain places.

Please be aware of these sensations, make a mental note and see if there is any commonality or correlation to these occurrences.

There are so many so-called experts on You Tube, so many saying that they are connected and that they know things, that they are here to teach you how to get to know your loved ones and other spirits. Unfortunately, there are charlatans and fakes but we have no way of letting you know that these people are coming from a place of ego and power. The power because they want to tell people that they are different and have this skill but please be careful of these as they can give wrong information and instructions. When trying to find out more about us through You Tube be discerning. Don't take anything on face value. Always be a little sceptical, always ask questions. We want you to notice what you feel when listening to these things. What part of the body does it affect? Remember we talked about the somatic sensory system in your body. Go back to the chapter and practice some more if you have forgotten.

Sit, listening to the output from the clip, close your eyes and see what you feel around the body. Do you have your truth detector turned on? Everyone will come across someone fake at some time. There are a lot of them; people advertising on the internet for horoscope readings, spirit readings, tarot readings and they charge a lot of money. Sometimes these charlatans are very clever and have been practicing for a while to give overall general advice. Even the telephone conversations you can have from mediums can fool you. If these people have been through trauma themselves, they are often attracted to these types of professions. Because they have been hurt, they are on their journey to heal. A lot of people go into the healing arts because they want to be healed. Generally, this isn't the best way to do this. First repair and get over the trauma as much as possible, love yourself and deal with all your hidden demons.

Sometimes these practitioners come from a place of hurt, they will always put their own spin on it. There are certain key phrases that people use:

I see you have had a few hurts in the past perhaps with family or a close friend. Really who hasn't by the time they reach adulthood.

There is an influential man coming into your life or has been, how was that for you? There is often a prominent man in most people's lives — this is not special.

I see that you have money problems in the past and may have been taken advantage of. Again, who hasn't? If you are rich then of course there will be money problems, either from overspending or a business deal gone wrong. And if you have no money then yes you probably have.

There is someone trying to reach you from the other side, a grandparent, have they passed over? Here they are scratching at something about a loved one. And most grandparents have passed over or they will say it's your great grandparent.

If they ask these kinds of general questions, then they are fishing. It is best if they can mention something specifically about you or your past loved one. If that person is communicating with them, they can stipulate certain things, like an ornament, or a clothing item or a specific event. Be cautious before you hand over any money. The best way is to have a recommendation or go to a direct channeler, either through these records or book an appointment to see someone that reads these Akashic Records

(The place where all soul files past, present and future of this earth and beyond, are kept, they are in another dimension and this book comes from them) or channels with another person coming into their body. You will know. If unsure then ask someone you trust implicitly about these matters.

The medium should come from pure love and helping of humanity. Have a proven record of their skills, perhaps even give you numbers of people who they have read for and check up on them. If they are genuine, they will happily give you a couple of numbers after their permission has been given to do so. Or several of your friends have already been. It's always worth a background check.

Try different people on You Tube, test them, try the meditations or the chakra balancing. Try them, what do you feel? Did it sit well with you? There are many different people and many different ways of doing the same thing. Work out what is right for you. Don't always believe what you read on the internet as they may not be coming from Source. It is the true word from Source. The Akashic Records have every single soul's journey in the files there. As well as souls from other planets and universes. This is a direct dial to Source through these records. Others have used us from the records like Rudolf Steiner, the Austrian Philosopher. The Records are referred to in his writings. The Alcoholic Anonymous guide to staying sober was also channelled from Source — from us. Bill Wilson and Dr Bob Smith wrote the 12 steps through wisdom and experience. We brought observations and ideas through dreams from the higher power, from us. These two are perfect examples of what was written — works. It is tried and tested and still going. AA is still doing great work with people in recovery from addiction and the schools that teach children first art and expression before reading and writing also works really well although not for all children as no one thing suits everybody.

We ask that you take your time in assessing which is the right way for you to do. The Akashic Records have your soul's journey, past and future, written. Your soul's journey is staying on your path and not falling off and serving the ego. If possible, stay on your contract — listen to your teacher and master, and grow spiritually and wholly. Everybody slips off the path and that is good, otherwise you do not learn the contrast of what flows and what doesn't. If you fall away from the contracts' path then things get convoluted and changed, nothing flows that you plan but the process of allowing and patience will keep you on the path. The Akashic Records have the path written down in a file and can be tapped into via us — we are all, we are loved ones of yours, we are interplanetary beings, we are great leaders (see the list of Ascended Masters) there are more than on the list, many more but there is only so much space we can list them on. We are all that you want us to be. We know the truth of the universe, we know everything about you, we know everything that may or may not happen. Please ask us for guidance, we are here to help and we come from a place of love. If you want to ask for help for others, we are more than happy to help. If it is something big or they are enquiring about something or even us then you need to get their permission in order for us to fully help. Remember visibility and truth are what we work from as we want you to.

Do not keep volunteering offers of reading cards, or Psychometry, or aura reading unless they are ready and want to do it. Wait to be asked; it is their contract not yours. You can explain what you are learning, and offer, but do not push the point.

Be kind, be compassionate for those who have lost their beloveds, be genuine and sincere to help those who are hurting. Gentleness is the key.

We love you, we love all.

Go in peace through the day.

And so it is…

24.

Tarot
by Oshun

We want to share with you the use of tarot cards. They came about when a long time ago people wanted to converse with us and through symbolism, we were able to get messages across. Ancients previously used bones, imagery, and specially prepared herbs to ingest to get closer or to channel our messages. Tarot is to help people be aware of any problems that may arise. Some cards that help people look at themselves and the message that we want to get through. It makes people be aware of their true self by having them contemplate what we have put in front of them through cards to help them make the right decisions. Messages also help cement what you already know deep down. They are also a playful way of an introduction to our world and the world of light workers and evolved human beings.

They come in many different styles. Many have channelled the pictures and the explanations were also channelled with other evolved humans. They are like a pack of cards with what you call the Arcane. There are the 22 major Arcane and the minor arcane. The 22 tell you of major things that you need to be aware of. What they mean right side up and reverse. Generally, the pictures that have been channelled are significant in the drawing. All the small parts of the picture can be interpreted to mean something. Some packs are beautiful, and others are clever in their interpretation. All basically have the same meaning and the reader needs to hone their skills in order to channel what is coming through. The minor Arcane are about everyday lives of humans and how things need to be considered when moving forward through life. These too are beautiful in their presentation. There are many that come from different countries and all have their particular style. Some countries have themes of their folk lore. These tarots, are one of the longest standing skill set known to mediums and clairvoyants. Originally mentioned in The Book of Thoth, the God of wisdom, He had his priests inlay pictures onto plates providing imagery for tarot.

Etteilla findings for the Egyptian tarot 1789 https://www.mentalfloss.com/article/71927/tarot-mythology-surprising-origins-worlds-most-misunderstood-cards

The minor Arcane include wands (will, fire), swords (power/intellect, Air), cups (emotions, water) and pentacles (physical, earth). They all have separate meanings. The symbolism is particular to the set that you have started to use. (Table as quick reference in glossary)

If you are getting some for yourself then be aware of the higher self, directing you to a pack. You may be drawn and it catches your eye. Look at them all to feel the energy of each pack. What do you notice? Do you keep coming back to the same pack? If so, then that is the one for you. If you are buying for someone else then do the same. Think about that person before you get to the shop or are buying online. Think of them, think of their personality and when you get there, tune into your friend and feel how they are. Stand in the shop and feel the packs energetically. Which are you drawn to? Whichever pack has the most drawing of your attention then these are the ones. You have to trust.

There are other kind of packs called the Oracle cards and these work in a slightly different way but essentially are the same and the messages will come through, no matter what pack you decide to buy. With the Oracle cards there are less of them but there are often more explanations with each card. The upright, the reverse, the significance of asking about a relationship, and the significance of asking about money and abundance. Not all packs have this but we leave it to your honing skills to read it from your nothingness.

There are particular ways of setting out the cards and the meaning to them. There are tried and tested patterns illustrated in the handbook that comes with the cards. There are also different ways of reading the cards. Generally, the past is first then the present and then the future, near, soon and far away. This is true also for past events, recent past and long-time past. Practise to see what fits your style.

Another way not mentioned in most books is a nine-card spread. Three cards to the left is past, three cards above is present and three to the right is the future. The middle card of each set of three is the main event and either card around it is about the event. Try this way and see what comes out as well.

You can also read your own cards every day to see how your life is. It is not necessary to do a seven, nine, or 12 card spread but instead do a quick three or one card to help you through your day.

Play with them, get familiar with them. Feel the cards and what do you see. Hold each card when reading. If you don't get an immediate answer, put the card in one hand and the other place on top and see what comes up in your nothingness. Be still and quiet and things will appear. At first when practicing read the book of explanations and as you get better and more familiar then things will become easier. And as we have stated before practice, practice, practice.

Be careful of your explanation and interpretation as this is always subjective, not objective unless you are truly practice and evolved. Things come from experience in your interpretation. From your own experiences so you have your own trauma or episodes of good and bad and may draw from your experiences and may not necessarily realise that you are not completely impartial.

Things that are stated in readings like this can also be changed by choices and pathways. If something bad has come up and it is in the future then personal choices may not always lead to that bad event. But instead have been forewarned so the events leading up to it are all human choice and subjective in observation. If it is in your contract to go through this then by being warned you can either minimise the occurrence or redirect your life by making another choice. Tarot cards are good at warning people and they can set in place alternatives, whatever they may be.

Life is not set in stone as we gave you choice to work through your contracts as well as free will. It just depends on you how you manage these choices. Also remember to listen to your teacher and master (soul and heart) and what they are telling you. Some clairvoyants just use these cards as a tool but they are really a medium that can tune into your energy and past life(s).

For practiced clairvoyants or mediums that are genuine and skilled they should be able to tell you of a past event in your life. This gives you an idea of how genuine they are. Also do your own card readings often — does it change? Or are the readings generally along the same lines. As we said play with them. They are fun. And always remember that it is the readers' interpretation and therefore not necessarily the gospel of your life. Have fun, laugh and practice.

We are with you in the readings but don't forget to ask.

Go in love…

25.

Death
by Arnoah

We are here to talk about death and how it happens. People are often afraid of death and the passing of their
body and soul into the next. However, many do not believe that there is another life and another life and another life. So it goes on, until all the lessons have been experienced and learnt from these lives. Many people do not believe this, yet we would like to bring a few things to your attention to help give depth to the theory of reincarnation. This theory has been proved several times (Dr Ian Steveson claimed to have 3000+ cases of reincarnation and shared with the scientific community. *Reincarnation and Biology: A Contribution to the Etiology of Birthmarks and Birth Defects* (1997).) but others do not think that there is sufficient evidence. The written word by the Buddhists have shown that reincarnation is real. They preach or follow the scripture that has been written by many past Buddhas. Their process of their belief system is that humans come into this earth with a knowledge of what went on in their past lives. By this we mean the contract has been written that the soul will gravitate towards the professions that they have already been working in. The contract that they want to work out in this life has been communicated with us and the soul. People have a propensity to go towards what they know. New professions take a little longer to learn. For example, a natural born athlete that you see in their field of sport is hugely talented. What has been before is that person probably did sports in many other lives and is continuing the thing that the soul loves. Jumping high, running fast, swimming like a dolphin are all very natural skills that these people have. Only because they have done it before. It's the same with other professions, cooking, accounting, building and all

the other professions in life. The soul will gravitate towards them, as they are familiar and the soul may want to try and make a success of their profession in this life so they stick with what they know and love.

The Buddhists have been trusting this process as explained earlier.

This shows that a reincarnation occurs and that you all go through this process in becoming who you are, what you become great at and how to conduct your life.

Have you ever wondered why certain things feel really familiar but haven't been there before? You get a sense that all around seems comfortable or relaxed as if you have been there before. Well the chances are that you have. Déjà Vu is an occurrence when the soul has actually already been there and life is catching up to the soul, and that you are where you are supposed to be at that time and that your life is on the right path. It's a joining of energy of your lives of what is about to happen with what is happening. Déjà vu is just a time glitch as your soul re-joins the energy of your life.

Do you get déjà vu much? Does it happen when you least expect it? Or do you even notice or shrug it off as just being weird? Yes, it is weird as there was also a glitch in what you assess as time. Time is an interesting construct that humans have made in order to create world order. We get that. We will explain time in more detail later.

Do you ever have a sense of knowing someone when you meet them for the first time? Yet really you have never met them at all in your lives. You get on well and you both seem familiar to each other and neither can put your finger on it. In fact, it may be quite obsessive not knowing when you met that person. After a while neither of you can figure out whether you have met each other before. If that is the case you have connected before in another life.

People who have died and come back on the operating table speak of wondrous things on the other side. They speak of seeing the light, a beautiful light that is coming closer to them to assist them to the other side - Source. This is where they can repair, get stronger and become at peace with themselves. All burning questions are answered over here that humans have. Especially those who are atheists, they really get a shock. Once here at Source you realise that there is so much here; love, kindness, friendship, knowledge, being, acceptance of all. There is no prejudice, anger, hate, guilt and sadness. There may be hurt and anger at first as they believe that they have gone before their time. This rarely happens as most natural deaths are planned and written into your contract. However, suicide is not a natural death and is not written into any contract. Suicide is about the choices you have made through your lives. Your path has got rocky and certain choices have taken you away from the path and then things start to spiral out of control.

Another possibility is that an entity has latched on to that sad person and is making them worse than ever before. They lock into the negative emotions that people feel and don't let go unless somebody sees them and deals with them accordingly.

Suicide is difficult, not only for the loved ones around them who are left behind but also difficult later for the person who took their own life. Unfortunately, because the time of death has been changed from the correct time of death, which could be six months from now, it could be 10 years from now but the person and soul has to wait in a place until the right time of death has come. It is a terrible shame that there are so many youth suicides as these young souls have to wait. It is like a small sub-group away from Source but still connected to Source, like a subsidiary company we believe you will understand. We look after these souls and give them love and kindness. While they wait, we also teach and give them lessons on aspects of their lives to help them know better and the triggers for their next life. We teach them how to detect and avoid entities. We teach them a new way of loving. In their lives they experienced a bad kind of love, a selfish kind of love. One that may have brought a sexual abuser to their bed when they were young, this was not their contract and neither was it the abuser's. They left their path and had been coerced or tempted by excessive hedonism. The ego took over and unless those humans are strong and can see what they are doing is wrong the ego will continue to control them. The teacher and master are muted and suppressed — almost like being held prisoner. The busy lives that you have make it so the ego has a bigger playground, as there is very little reflective time, and listening time to your heart and soul. Always busy and rushed and of course stressed in this modern way of life.

Other proof that reincarnation, many lives and Source exist is that souls are born of the same family and have traits of the passed loved one.

Often a grandfather or another dearly loved elder that has passed, or even an untimely death (or so you think) will be reincarnated into the family again. You can realise this when the child begins to grow and you listen to them, they can be wise beyond their years or they have a trait that is very much like the past loved one's. Or they gravitate towards the loved one's profession – walking in his grandfather's footsteps for example. Again, this is the subtle truth that Source and all of us do exist and that the ones who see us, hear us, or feel us are not crazy, they just see the real truth.

Many are scared and some welcome death. The ones who are scared, what are you scared of? The unknown of where you the soul is going? or that you will miss your loved ones here on this earth? or that you haven't accomplished everything you wanted to do? The bucket lists humans have are well worth doing as you never know when it will happen. It's about having the soul experience many things and feeling different places. The pyramids and Machu Picchu are places of great vibration. Listen to your soul and where it takes you. Either places with feelings or have experiences that evoke feelings. All of this is learning. Don't waste days that you may regret. Live life to the full so that you have no regrets. Obviously if you wanted to be president of a country and it didn't happen for that go easy on yourself as there are only so many of you that can rule a country. We mean things like travel, or visiting relatives across the world, or let bygones be bygones with a close friend or family. Don't carry over with you too many regrets, in fact ideally you would have no regrets. If you followed your heart and soul in all that you did at the time of that decision, then regrets are futile and not necessary. You did everything you wanted, right?

If you are afraid of death because you will miss your loved ones, remember that you can hang out with them while they go about their daily business. You can help them in their daily lives, and decisions. You will contact them through electricity or once you have been here and practiced you will even be able to move things and place objects elsewhere just to let them know you are around.

We are waiting for your transition to Source with unbounded love. We notice and observe that your religions books say that we judge. We only have acceptance to all of you no matter what you have done in your lives. Please be rest assured there is no judge or jury and pearly gates, you all come to the same place of energy and the mistakes that you have made will be talked about, learnt about and the reasons why so that the soul can go on to the next life and work through what they did in the past life. Also, acceptance that karma will teach you of your misgivings on earth and we hope that the soul will learn in the next life. Notice these lessons and be retrospective about how not to make the same mistakes. Otherwise, the lessons can get really repetitive.

Death is not something you should be afraid of, but it takes a lot of belief and conviction in what you have learnt from us and your belief in Source. Again we reiterate; there is no judgement, you will not be refused "entry". No matter what you know you have done. Remember, it's about the long picture not the short gains. It's always for the greater good. The skills you have learnt on this earth and up in Source will help you make the right decisions for yourself in your next life and train you to listen to the heart and soul more often. Gradually as you go through your lives learning it will become easier to follow your true self, your authentic self and then the lives will only get better every time. Just be careful of the ego and entities.

Go in love, have love for all and you will learn and accept just as we accept everything about all of you.

We love you always…

Amen.

26.

Others
by Arnoah

We want to talk to you of us. Who we are and where we come from. My name is Arnoah and I am from the Leberia. We as a race roam throughout the universes and help civilisations to find a better way of operating and running a planet. Some other planets similar to yours have gotten the hang of acceptance and non-judgement but just like the human race it has been a long hard struggle for the evolved amongst them. From the planet Turia there were civil wars, revolutions and suppression of the masses. Through peaceful demonstrations and new generations, the people got stronger and refused to vote for the old paradigm and old ways. The leaders of Turia were eventually overpowered and the new generation started to govern. It took some time — over decades in your timing. Gradually, as the people grew in awareness and kindness, they realised there was another way. Telepathy was developed, people started to meditate more over the years, their knowledge became really in tune with each other so that they were then able to communicate with others without getting caught by the officials. The parents showed the children — young ones, how to meditate and concentrate for the greater good. It was introduced in what you call schools. Gradually, over the years there was more and more silent communications. More and more of them began to believe in us, Source and the greater good. Their world was starting to break down, and more and more pressure was put on the manufacturing to make more money. Eventually there were very little worldly supplies and a new way had to be found.

Their governments started storing food for the people but really kept it for the select few. The corrupt at the top, the greedy and the selfish. The masses got wind of this, especially when the food supplies were dwindling, and hunger was becoming widespread. The people started to use their skills in telepathy. They came together and the food supplies around their planet were then accessed. The powers that be were voted out and the new order took over. Supplying all the people the food and began true sustainability for all. The food was shared out in rations and the masses were saved. Now in Turia, the people work with each other and nobody goes hungry. There now is no greed because the stories of the elders talk of the deprivation and starvation that the past leaders put upon them. New governance was written to help all the people. Money became secondary and all are fed throughout Turia.

What this example shows is that there is another way once the Earth has reached its extremes. We hope that this will not be so for humankind. We hope that the world leaders will come together to make sure that this doesn't happen. We are not sure if Gaia can keep going with all the pillaging that you humankind do. The greed for more and more wealth is all consuming for some in Gaia. As we have said before these are young souls that will need more lessons to show them that the greater good is far more a worthwhile cause than lining their own pockets.

Sadly, these lessons can take time as the powerful don't want to lose control.

In order to have true control you actually need to relinquish control and trust us that it will all work out in the end. However, with this belief system you have to be really trusting of Source and all that that entails. You relinquish your control and allow things to happen the way it should be, but this does not mean that a world with a selfish, greedy leader will get what they ask for. They are not coming from a place of love and integrity. Instead they have to relax and allow the way for the greater good. The Law of Attraction will help with your requests because it is a universal law. Money does attract money you have seen this in the stock markets however there are times when everything will be lost. A person loses all this money and wealth and has to start again. We want these people to really change their way of thinking, learn by the crash of the market and learn that being without money is not as bad as it seems. It is harder if you have been wealthy but are then thrown into poverty, or what they would consider poverty. Actually, it could be a normal life, like the majority of people. Catching the bus, walking to places, buying food at the supermarket and watching what you spend. This is a well-earned lesson for the richer of you. To be experiencing the normal life of the majority. Many lessons are learnt when thrown into poverty; compassion, selflessness, kindness, and acceptance. Hopefully, the person will not get resentful and mean but instead learn how others live. If they do not learn this then it will be repeated.

Money (energy) can be used for a great many things, it doesn't necessarily mean that it is bad and dirty instead one can share the wealth that has been made and put it to good use. There are several in your world that do this. They have great wealth and they are sharing. If only more would do this as there is a finite number of objects that you can actually buy and be happy. Some of you think that being wealthy will make you happy. This isn't so. The happiness only lasts for a little while. Happiness comes from within. How you feel is what really counts. Happiness and contentment are what you should be striving for. This brings health to every cell in your body. This helps the immune system, this helps you sleep better, this helps everyone around you. Others see your happiness and wants a piece. This is your chance to share your experiences and how you came to be that content.

The vibration of happiness resonates at a higher frequency. The cells vibrate in a subtle way. Those of you who are more evolved will see this or feel it. Others who are younger may not but will realise there is something different about them. We find that the person who has handed over their control to us and aren't trying to force events or experiences to happen but allows things to unfold. To trust implicitly is the key. We will deliver your desires but at the point of time when it is most appropriate. This is where the control has been given up and allowance and acceptance of the timing is everything. Patience is often a lesson to be learnt here.

There are those of you that have everything that they desire and more, they seem the lucky ones. They are the person who travels through life with everything that they need. Doors just open for them when they want or close to it. If it doesn't happen straight away for them then they wait as they know in their heart and soul that it will happen. The trust or rust moment. However, for these people they still have to work through some other lessons, work through personal relationships, emotional hardships in this life, rather than career and money abundance. These people have complete and utter trust in the process of the universal laws. They don't let negative thoughts in, they remember to ask for what they want and they wait until it happens; and it does happen. At the appropriate time at in the flow.

The ones who are afraid of losing their money, probably will. They have had that thought which puts a vibration into the universe and therefore it continues in the same way. The hard part is keeping the faith and not giving up. To have trust in the fact that it will happen. We do deliver but often just at the crucial moment. We are not trying to test your faith, it is just how it is.

If you drop a thought or request for something that you need it is like a pebble into a lake and you watch the ripples extend outwards, this is how a thought occurs with a request. The bigger and with more conviction the thought; the ripples will be more defined. Be careful what you ask for.

Contentment and happiness are key, and the more you exude this, the more people will want to know you. With contentment and happiness there is less anger, hurt, and worry. Eventually it becomes easier and the snowball of happiness gets bigger and bigger. Your light starts to shine through and your evolvement continues to return to Source if that is your request having learnt and remembered your lessons or experiences.

The more people that recognise kindness the more it will become like an infectious disease and spread. Smiles are infectious, people can't help smiling back at you. Vibrations of the higher resonance are oozing out of your very being and aura. People gravitate towards this. Please be kind to others as this gathers great vibrations and if more people are vibrating at that level then it can raise the vibration of Gaia. This is the ultimate goal. Gaia will be saved, the corrupt greedy leaders will fall away and genuine people will start governing the countries with integrity and truth. We welcome this but understand as we said before it will take several generations for the new order to really take hold.

We love you, we support you, believe and trust it will happen.
And so it is.

27.

Solace and Symbols by Isis and Arnoah

We want to talk to you today about solace with calmness when all those about you are losing their heads.

There is calmness once you have practiced meditation. People around sense this and gravitate towards you. We look on Gaia as a beautiful calm planet but once you scratch the surface things are not what they seem. The world leaders are coercing and plotting for their own wealth and gains. This is how it is right now and as we said before this will change slowly.

There are symbols and messages we want to bring to you and they help with universal healing and repairing places, not only for mankind but Gaia herself. These symbols have power when there is the intent of laying them on the body. They can also help by placing the Gaia symbol in areas of high vibration around the world, Stonehenge, Bolivia in the plateaus, The Black Forest in Germany, Ayres Rock in Australia and the Grand Canyon in the United States. These places have a high vibration already and by placing this Gaia symbol with your intent can help raise the vibrations of the Earth. It is the pebble in the lake phenomenon, the drop of a pebble — the intent of the symbols, and watch the ripples of the water expand out further and further until the ripples have reached the edge. This is the same for this Gaia symbol, lay it in the centre and allow the intentions to ripple out and help the areas. If you can have 528 Hz playing whilst doing this either out loud or in your ears (headphones) and allow the healing tone to extend with the ripples it will be more effective If you light workers and earth lovers work in this way then it will help Gaia to come right. The politics will start changing and the vibrations will begin to resonate higher. In your meditation visualise the symbol for Gaia in the centre of the world and gradually extend it out and up through the inside of the planet. Allow a purple flame through it and expand to the surface of the earth. Hold that visual for a few minutes. This will start to help in a small way. If more do this so the energy will raise up the vibration of healing to help earth.

You can also use these symbols to help people in their healing process. If colleagues are struggling at work then you can put a picture of the symbol on their desk, or you can tell them it will help and let's give it a try. You can photocopy these symbols and place them around you too if there is a hiccup in your energy. Perhaps as healers you can put the symbols up around the room and have clients stare at the particular symbols that correspond to the part of the body that is in pain.

The practitioner says these words to begin to open the channels of Divine energy. "Great Divine Spirit, Father, Mother God, Divine Angels of Divine Light. I welcome you into this room to help (*name of person being healed*) to be healed on many levels. I thank you, Amen."

Rub the palms of your hands together to stimulate the nerves. Holding your hands above the area of pain and using the corresponding symbol for that part of the body, imprint the symbol in your visualisation on that part of the body, allowing the energy of the Ancients to come through your head, down your arms and into the body. You may experience heat or coolness from the palms of your hands. The person may also experience the movement of energy. Keep with it until you are guided to move somewhere else. Or the sensation stops, or if you feel bored then it's time to move on to another part. Feel where the energy is guiding you, feet, head, belly and hold there. You will know, just trust your higher self.

These symbols are universal symbols of healing and light and we would love you to encompass them into your practice to help others. When wandering out in the bush or the countryside imprint these symbols from your mind with intent into areas that are being polluted and need help. Using the Gaia symbol or the Universal healer.

The land in Gaia is being polluted with chemicals which contaminates the food; with all the pesticides and herbicides to help grow the crops in order to stop pests devouring the crops. There are so many natural remedies for these crops that don't need these chemicals but instead using garlic, or certain oils sprayed on the crops can help keep little armies at bay. What humans have now come up against are super armies of the aphids, green fly, rust, moulds which have got stronger and now aren't affected by these toxic manmade pesticides. This is much like hospital super bugs where antibiotics just don't work anymore. The same are for the crops. There are many different remedies to help save the crops and make them more nutritionally viable for the body. These chemicals start to clog up your livers and kidneys, slowing them down over the years, and the brain with the heavy metals used in some of these solutions that are sprayed. Eventually the human body absorbs these and cannot always metabolise and flush them out, instead the heavy metals get deposited in the brain and diseases like Alzheimer's and motor neurons start affecting the human cells. Your healers have ways with herbs and tinctures to be able to get these metals out of the body towards better health. Unfortunately people don't realise the slow decline that the body is going into through the years and humans think it is just old age. Not necessarily. These chemicals build up in the body and slow everything down. Again, as we said before this is a long slow way of keeping the activists weak and non-effectual. The way that sugar has taken over is incredible and that the taste buds are changing towards more sweet foods. The processed sugar is detrimental to the body. Sugar encourages inflammation in the body. Diabetes is growing in the community along with obesity and cardio problems, and are not so strong to fight and stand up for human rights. The corn syrup that is in a lot of manufacturing is addictive and affects the brain through the dopamine pathway. It is incredible that large corporations feed children this in fast foods. It is very clever in making more money but in the end, it will cost more through hospitals, diseases of the autoimmune systems and they will continue to treat with manmade drugs.

    A lot of diseases can be combated using herbs, foods and other therapies, and it would be great if more people went to their local healers. They still do in villages around the world in underdeveloped countries, their local "witch", village doctor, herbal woman or by another name are at one with the Earth, the recipes have been handed down through the generations and work with Gaia, not against it. They also have an understanding that the healing crisis is not smooth and pain free, but instead a fever will have to be broken, the leg to be reset if broken and a purge if you have been poisoned is also necessary. These ancients have an understanding in the process of these things but in the Western world people don't want to go through anything that maybe painful. We agree you shouldn't have to, but in the way disease works, some uncomfortable sensations may have to be experienced in order to get healthy. We do agree pain for the sake of pain is unnecessary and some of the practitioners do have a sinister side. The first rules of your doctors are: do no harm. However, some do not follow this rule. Pharmaceutical drugs can do a lot of harm and are often unnecessary.

If the farmers didn't treat the food products badly (using chemicals and herbicides) then there would be less disease. If there was less stress in everyday life then less people would get sick. Cancer wouldn't be on the rise and other auto immune diseases. Vaccinations can take its toll on a young baby as well. We understand why you do this, and you believe for the greater good, but it is also a money-maker for the pharmaceutical companies. If you believe in vaccinations that is fine however if you could leave it until the child is at least two and a half then their little immune systems have a better chance of dealing with the side effects and would be more robust. Or better still five years old. Some childhood diseases should be gotten, measles, mumps, chicken pox, and scarlet fever. These help build up the child's immune system for later if other diseases are around and their constitution will be stronger. Children should play in the dirt, sand and forests and should get mucky and have fun. If they are happy children then the disease won't take hold so well and the child will fight it off just as nature intended. Unfortunately, even chemicals used for cleaning houses are breaking down the immune system as these small particles of cleaning materials get into your food and respiratory system and again slowly compromises your health.

Your children are your future and we wish you would stop poisoning them in the under-hand way that the large companies are doing. In the supermarket, on television, with marketing and it becomes the norm so people don't think it is strange any more. With all the stress and busy lives, you don't have the time or the energy to fight back, or not buy certain products. The fresh organic produce is expensive but if every farmer used organic pesticides and cleaned up their land then the prices would come down. The chemical fertilisers wouldn't need to be bought and the natural way would suffice. If you are a farmer, then you can grow crops that produce natural pesticides, for example, grow a small patch of garlic, or oregano, thyme, parsley and many more that are natural plant protectors and the cost would be brought down. There would be more employment in the farming industry rather than the manufacturing industry. The people would be working outside instead of in factories or chemical plants, all would still have employment it would be in a different industry and less harmful. Air-conditioned factories spread disease too. Instead out in the sunshine, with good air eventually. There would be produce in the markets grown with integrity and kindness. The produce takes on the energy of the farm. So, you would be eating happy produce. Just like happy free-range meat. It makes your bodies feel good. Chemicals, sugar, processed foods do not help the body feel good. Think about what you are consuming.

Look after yourself as much as you can, feed yourselves and your children with more whole foods, less chemicals, less fast foods, and they will grow strong, clever and full of energy to be able to make a difference. Don't let the chemical system keep you down, start changing little by little and try to eat fresh as much as possible. If organic is out of your price range at the moment then just eat fresh and be as happy as you can be.

Again, as we have said before meditate, this helps to keep you happy, stay on your path of kindness, compassion, lessons, acceptance and non-judgement and your body shouldn't get sick. If you do contract a disease especially if written in your contract then look after yourself or have someone care for you. Don't feel guilty about asking someone to help even if you rarely do this. Givers find it hard to receive remember... is this you? Others are happy to take care of you we are sure, if they have the time. Community and family are key. This is solace... to be comforted by loved ones.

Love, light and healing to all.

Complete Body

Universal Healing

Kidneys

Hands

Lower Back

Blood

Auras

Upper Back

Heart

Head Face

Pelvis

Lungs

Gaia

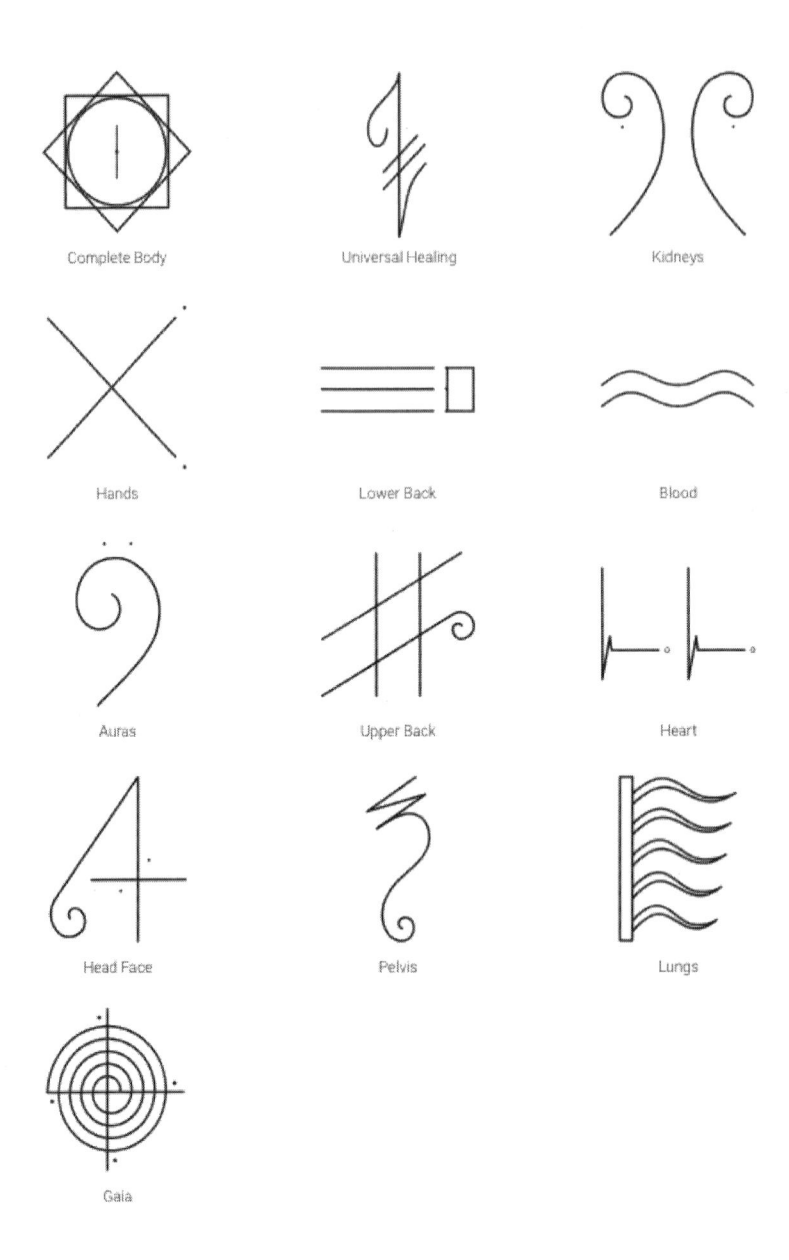

Interplanetary symbols to facilitate and heal body parts and energies. ©
The Connection Collection ©

28.

Hello and Explanations by Arnoah

We have spoken to you of many things, about corruption, about food industries, about love, relationships and human emotion. We hope that you are meditating and learning to use your senses to move through space and interact with others.

We hope that you are feeling calmer and more peaceful and are learning the true meaning of acceptance of what is around you in your day. We spoke to you of who we are and how we are channelling through her the author. We come through the Akashic records and the divine. We are united with others from different universes and other interplanetary galaxies. We come in love first and foremost and we want the best for you and your learning.

What we see is essentially love and kindness throughout your world but it is heavily laden with emotions of the ego and cruel people. This is challenging for the light workers and others who are enlightened and evolved. The strength within yourselves is often challenged and questioned by the others. There are millions of you all at different stages of evolvement and are moving through your lives as best you know how, as well as those who do not believe you have a soul. You are still evolving but you are not aware of the big picture yet and total global unity. This is fine for the new young souls as we have said before, they need to find out whom and what they are, but this can take several lives. These are the people that go through life being all about them. There is very little gratitude and service in their lives, have more a sense of entitlement. But as it is written they will come back to do service to mankind eventually.

There are theories in these passages that have information about global change. For many believe this cannot happen as there are too many obstacles right now. We can see how you would think this way, however, everything takes time and once all the communication avenues are open then more global unity will start to form. The global leaders will see that there is more communication amongst people from other countries. New groups are being formed with common interests of spiritual awareness globally. You can now have discussions and meetings with people and other souls to start getting stronger for the new order. The older light workers are diligent in their work of unity. More practitioners and therapists are starting to join forces and hold evenings of music, tones and chanting. Often like the ancients had done. Civilisations of the Incas and Native North Americans practiced this way. Often sending themselves into a frequency of delirium and chanting. The vibrations of the instruments played for a period of time starts to vibrate through the body and its cells, all the way into the bones and organs. By having these sessions to raise their vibrations so they were able to meditate at a higher frequency. Thus, being able to communicate with us on another level and we are then able to give messages to the elders to help and teach humans about Gaia. Unfortunately, as time went on, science started to take over. In the newly formed universities, all over the world science became more important. Even religions started to take up science to explain things of the scriptures. The pendulum swung all the way over to the other side where it became wrong to believe in spirituality and science was the only answer for proving things in your world. You are always looking for a reason that things happen. There are still miracles going on but not so much in the Western world but more in countries that still have a great spiritual presence; India, China, Pakistan, Lao, Philippines, Australia and the civilisation of the Inuits, so far are still holding their own when it comes to spirituality. The South Americans also have a huge spiritual belief. The Inuits are very spiritual people and have managed to stay that way as there is very little interference from the Western world. There are many of these sub-cultures that carry on the ancients' work in their community. Indigenous people are the most spiritual. These communities generally have a medicine man, or women that take care of the people in the village or township. They also have a sensitive side in seeing us or other loved ones that help their village. These kinds of people are often skilled as it is passed down their blood line and these skills are learnt from a very early age. The apprenticeship is started early and children train alongside the elders. They are taught all that they know and that their ancestors have known.

There were many Western explorers that went to these lands and tried to take over. To put their 'superior' way of life on to them. They raped and pillaged these cultures as the Western ego for power and money took over. Stripping their lands of the precious stones, silks and spices as well as abusing the local villages for their own selfish end. The famous explorers Columbus and Cook, both devastated lands of the South Pacific and abused the locals, yet in Western history books these men were seen as heroes. Thankfully now the books report how actually they were intoxicated with wealth and power, then took what they wanted, when they wanted with no cost. With guns as their weapons the indigenous people had no way of fighting back. Then there was the slavery movement where again the 'white superior race' saw these cultures as lesser beings. Thankfully, this is not so anymore but so much damage has been done. However, there are some that are not letting this go and always live in the past and the past wrongs that were done to the people. That is past now, long time past yet many are not able to let some things go. This is unhealthy as it means acceptance hasn't fully occurred. These are lessons that need to be learnt. Acceptance, a hard and powerful lesson. We agree things should be put right and compensation should be acknowledged but as with humans there is always someone that won't move on, stays in the pain of the past. What we also see is that even though the governments are trying to do the right thing and pay compensation that the leaders of those tribes or cultures are actually not letting the money filter down to the people. Instead these leaders of the cultures have also got the bug of greed and corruption. They have used some of the monies given to the tribe for their own personal gain. Have they not learnt from the white Western world model that it doesn't work? That this meanness and selfishness will eventually come out and the people that the monies were supposed to go to learn of the corruption and will revolt against their leaders.

This is what we mean that money and power can corrupt easily, especially if the leaders have never had that wealth and have always been struggling. All of a sudden, they have this income to dispose of, amounts for the people but they seem to cream off the top which makes them just as bad as everyone else. As we have said before it is the new up and coming leaders that will make a change. They will see that benefitting the people will give them more benefits of contentment, happiness, altruism, compassion and kindness. This is so much more rewarding to the soul that they will then vibrate at a higher frequency and good things continue to happen for everyone. This will take time as we have spoken before.

Keep practicing meditation; keep practicing kindness, compassion and acceptance. This will attract more of the same, Law of Attraction, it is inevitable. Kindness will grow, equality will grow.

And so it is…

29.

Advice
by Arnoah

We want you to understand how life works and the big picture. Life is valuable and worthwhile in what you can accomplish for others as well as yourself. There are things that are changing in the universes that surround your universe. There are many other life forms that haven't been discovered by humans yet.

We want you to know that there is a solution to the problems of the Earth — Gaia. We are here to help you and guide you to helping the world powers to become more sympathetic to one and all of their people and communities. We understand that there are more of you that want to help Gaia survive. This will happen as we said before — it will happen but slowly. Through the next few generations things will start to change. The people will start seeing what is really happening and the people will rise up and vote for the people they want to run their country. Corruption will start to diminish as the new stronger younger people come through to help the masses.

We see many great things happening and gradually things will start changing. The journalists through media will start to bring corruption to a head but this will take a while as the heads of state have been used to controlling the media in certain countries, for example, China, North Korea and Russia Now that there is social media where anybody can post things the truth will start to be revealed. Firstly, in small increments and people will gradually start putting the stories together. Then the people will figure it out. Their new world order will come to fruition and will start standing up for what they believe in. At first these will be quashed but the more people start to say something then there will be too many to follow up to stop them publishing. There will not be enough corrupt authorities to stop this movement.

Peaceful demonstrations are the way to go. Meditation and deliberation of yourselves and Gaia will help raise the vibration and subtly change the energies of this beautiful planet. We wish people would realise that the world doesn't revolve around them but actually revolves around the sun! We want you, through practice of service for mankind to show others how worthwhile it is and spread like a virus of good will.

These words are to encourage light workers and others to help spread the word of acceptance and non-judgement to help others to practice the same. With these skills that you have found in this book you will be able through demonstration to show others what is really possible. The resolute will keep going and practicing. Going out in this world and teaching others. There will be some that start with a hiss and a roar and then start to flail and lag and then perhaps stop. That is fine as now may not be the right time for them. Or their life is too busy to have the head space to start with meditation.

Families are important and caring for your loved ones, young and old. If this is how it is for you then wait til you have the time, perhaps when the children have grown up a bit more and they won't rely on you so much then this will be a good time. You need to have the headspace to do it. As well as the energy space. If your mind is busy with the everyday chores and duties and you have tried to settle it but it seems futile, give it another five minutes and see if you can settle your mind. As we said even if you feel it is useless just some of that time doing it will actually have some affect energetically.

If you feel you want to try meditation that is fantastic. Persevere and something will start changing. A time before you go to bed when the house is quiet is really good. Perhaps once the children have gone to school if you are a stay at home parent. The chores can always wait and will always be there. We are sure you can put everything off for at least 20 mins. Rationally think about it, you would spend 20 mins taking coffee with a friend. Or 20 mins doing the ironing, think of it this way, meditate as a process of self-preservation, of staving off sickness, to be internally content, to be able to not blow up at any little stress. To help your vibration rise and feel good, to have a more even personality, not fly off the handle, to be able to deal with stressful situations and keep your head to deal with the problem. People will start to notice the difference in you. Wouldn't you want to be like this? We know it seems daunting at first and nothing happens but with conviction for yourself to be healthier isn't it worthwhile?

It can be even simpler, try getting into bed and put a You Tube meditation or app. If you fall asleep that is fine too as it will still be affective even when you are sleeping. There are many that will suit most people. There are guided meditations with all sorts of stories and journeys. Or there are the ones with just pure sound. This can be harder at first to still the mind but guided will help you keep on track. And of course, don't get into conversation with the random thoughts. Tell yourself that you will get back to these issues once you are out of the meditation.

People who do meditate and have done so for a while begin to manifest whatever they want. Life goes more smoothly and less drama is in their lives. Don't you want this for yours? Alternatively, you can leave it until the children have gone and then get practicing. However, the many years you have not means you will have more practice to do. So why not just start attempting five days out of the seven or set yourself a challenge to do a complete month. Or at least 20 days out of the 30. You will notice a difference, not at first but gradually it will happen.

Please we ask you begin this meditation practice, but importantly do not beat yourself up if you do not do it. Guilt is not necessary as we do not judge, and we understand if it becomes too hard and the mental space and physical space is not there.

See what you can do as it will help on many levels, more than you could possibly imagine. The meditations that you humans do, affect Gaia in a beautiful way. She detects your vibrations and this helps her relax as well. The more that do it the more affect it will have on Gaia, you and all those around you.

We come in peace and tranquillity.

We have shown you the symbols, meditate on those as well, what we mean by this is have that symbol in front of you, turn on the tone and keep that picture in your mind's eye. Visualise the appropriate symbol placed on the body that you are trying to heal or yourself. Or have a symbol in your imagination for the world and meditate on that. What would be great for Gaia is to get a few friends over and have a meditation group together and put the symbol in the middle of the circle and meditate together. This is even more powerful. We know that some are doing this across the world and are joining together the power of healing on a massive scale. This is what we want to see more of. Talk about your spirituality with others and you will find more like-minded people than you think and they will begin to grow confidence as the law of attraction takes hold and the many come together for the greater good. Link in with other groups around the world and you will be amazed at the subtle changes that take place in not only your own vibrations, but of those who practice with you and Gaia. Good foundations of Gaia's energetic vibrations will help give stability and strong foundations of the new order coming to power. It will help avoid dramas on a grand scale and support Gaia going through the change of temperatures and change of landscapes.

We are here to support you light workers in your endeavours of love and unity.

All will be well…

30.

Conclusion
by Arnoah and Quan Yin

We see all, we see everything… we want you to know that you should not be hard on yourself when trying to get through this lifetime. And remember as you humans say you don't get out of life alive!

We would like you to start practicing all the lessons and knowledge we have given you. We want you to be aware of your feelings and adjust them accordingly to the situation. Don't let the emotions run away with you. Ground yourself, be your true authentic self, take some quiet time to go within. Book yourself time away from the family or work or friends and find some solace and gratitude for yourselves. Gratitude for who you are and what you are striving to be. Gratitude for many great and simple things. The smile of a child, the rising of the sun on such a beautiful morning, gratitude for your family, good or bad for they have helped you to mould and shape yourself to who you are today. You always have a choice no matter if you were put through a horrible childhood. Sometimes these lessons help shape you to be a great adult, an ability to learn from others and their bad decisions. If you were abused as a child or mistreated then rise above that abuse. Remember, it wasn't in your contract but you can turn it around and not continue the cycle. Instead treat your children with love and kindness. Remember, how it was for you as a child and change things. Violence is not okay and can be changed. Notice your patterns when bringing your own children up. Look at your behaviour. Are you going down the same way as your parents? Making the same mistakes that they did? Or do you get angry when your child frustrates you? Stop before you react. Take a breath, walk away from your child, calm down and notice how you are on the inside. Is your behaviour irrational? Don't rationalise violence towards your offspring. There are so many other ways. Remember children need boundaries.

Make them crystal clear so that the children know when they have stepped out of line. There are other ways of disciplining your children. Take something away that they want for a while. Some parents use a naughty chair. There are parenting help and guidelines written out there. Many books and help from professionals. Do not abuse children. Smother them with love and sensible boundaries. They will always challenge but that is how they learn. Let them make mistakes as they get older so that they can learn themselves. Even as parents you can teach but children don't always believe you or the outcome that you predicted. Instead allow them to figure it out. Watch quietly and pick up the pieces if there needs to be damage control. Remember the teenage years are when they start to come into their contract to learn. So again, they need to figure what is right for them or not.

Children are your future and if everything goes to plan, they will be running your world in a few decades. You have to shape their minds and the body to help save and preserve Gaia. You are their guardians to help them make a better world. They chose you — the parents. A world with very little violence (it will never ever truly be gone until mankind are all highly evolved beings — this will take centuries), a world where peaceful negotiations are the norm. Come to the negotiating table with love, compassion and with compromise in your mind in order to work out the best solution. What one may concede this time, then another may concede in another situation. Choose wisely and there will be results that both parties want. As with anything, it takes practice, sometimes humans learn slowly but we smile and know that you will eventually get it.

Reread the book, listen to the audio book again and feel the vibrations that we are sending with it. Allow those vibrations to impregnate into your very cells. The more you listen and continue with meditation the more understanding and comprehension you will have of this world and the bigger picture. With more understanding and the absorption of the truth so you will become calmer, find solace and compassion everywhere. Spirituality is everywhere. In everything you see. Love integrates into everything, you love yourselves, love everybody around (you may not like them right now) but love them and they will begin to feel the vibration.

Notice… learn… love… teach…

We come in peace.

31.

The Last Word by Arnoah

We want you to know the truth as it is revealed to you all. The truth is out there, and you have to go inside of yourself to detect the truth that is real. Many are scared of the truth because of the lies that they have built up within their lives. The stories, the pretence, the made-up rubbish that some think others want to hear.

We are watching over you all and the lies that people speak make us not only laugh but also cringe at what rubbish some spin. We find it hard to understand why so many do this yet if everyone spoke the truth then the low self-esteem, the insecurities of the self would not be so common. What do you have to hide? Have you some weird secret? If the secret does no harm to anyone in any way then it can stay a secret. You don't have to reveal all in this case. If you like dressing up in different clothes, or composing weird poetry for yourself then that is fine. We are talking about lies that affect others, the lies that do damage to others, the lies that are hurtful and meaningless. Stop it. Ask yourself the question of why do you do it? Why do you embed yourself into the web of deceit and lies? What does it get you in the long run? More money? More business? More social standing? Please just remember things always come out in the end. The truth will be revealed. Just like some politicians the unhealthy truth comes out when it's election time. The press goes digging to find stuff on the candidates. This is to ensure the integrity of the leaders. Sure, politicians spin great scenarios of their new government and what they can do for the people but gradually as it gets closer to the election the great promises get diluted. They speak of hopeful outcomes for the minority and hopeful outcomes for the majority but as you know not all can happen.

We have covered most of this before, but because lying is not being genuine, we wanted to mention it again. Please recap and reread. In fact, we would like you to read or listen often to these words to allow the vibration of what is to impregnate your very being. Gradually as you listen the energies will consolidate into your cells and begin to help you correct your behaviour to be with integrity, non-judgement and acceptance. The more you listen or read, the more you will learn. Just as with everything you learn you will only pick up what is right for you at that time in your life. Then let that lesson sink in, live with it and practice good compassionate behaviour. Once you are mostly confident in doing this then reread, or re-listen and see what else you have missed or picked up from these messages. There may be a phrase that you don't quite understand at first then you continue to read/listen and the explanation becomes more understandable. The truth of what we are speaking starts to affect you. You remember what we are teaching, and it becomes part of who you are.

Go to bed and read/listen to a chapter, feel the vibrations in the stillness of your body. Notice what part of your body or mind it may affect with the tone of the passage. Notice how you change over time and practice. Practice honing your skills and using your gifts. If you feel you do not have a gift then look again. Try different things, different skills, there are more than one mentioned in this book. Everyone has a slightly different gift, and at slightly different levels. We hope the ones that are more skilled can help the others that are not so. Please don't bring the ego in when helping a fellow light worker or apprentice as it is for the greater good. Showing integrity by teaching others means that you are becoming more evolved. The ones who do not want to share their skills and help teach then they are still struggling with the ego, and selfishness. If you are worried that they may take your clients, friends or skills — DON'T. This is a lesson that you need to learn. People who share skills, clients and friends are comfortable in where they are, have a knowledge that all will work out in the end and that what they are doing is for the greater good. This is the fundamental lesson we want you all to learn. For the greater good. To help people who are less fortunate than yourselves. This is being a light worker. This is what this is all about.

So plug in the audio book in the car, at night and listen again. Read late at night in the quiet. There will always be something more that you can learn or read/hear for the first time and truly understand it. And even once you think you have a handle on everything listen to it again. There is always something more. Many others reread the Bible or the Koran again and again and again. To the point where they live by the rules and understand the true meaning of their holy book. So reread this one and really feel the compassion, the kindness, and love vibrations that this book was written and channelled in. Feel us, feel yourselves growing and expanding. Be who you truly are. The soul will speak more often and you will be more aware of the messages that the teacher and master are telling you.

There is always free will so we can only recommend what to do with these words. You will know when to pick it up, listen carefully to your inner self and it will be a drawing towards what you need to do. You will know. Trust your soul.

We come in love.

32.

Leberia
by Arnoah

Lebarian is a race from a distant planet 140,000 light years away. We travel from there using light speed technology. We are tall beings and do not have a human face, our eyes are larger and one colour, no nose, and a little mouth. We are taller and more elongated than yourselves in the body. We speak very few words and instead use mainly telepathy. We have instant communication no matter how far away from each other we are. We have some hair which mainly grows from the back of our heads. We are also quite tall of about 2.5 meters or there abouts. We have glowing sensations around us that help communicate with others. This glowing is our auric field and is active by communicating with everything around us all the time. It is like another nervous system, which is how you would understand it. It is on the outside of our bodies but we also have a nervous system on the inside as well. The two communicate in unison and track all that is around us as well as interplanetary vibrations. This way we can feel troubled worlds and we can track them using this system around us. Our outside nervous system then is drawn to the vibrations of trouble. Often, we find that these kinds of vibrations are short and convoluted, no smoothness, just jagged and jarred vibrations. This is how we detected the problems in your world. The vibrations coming out of Gaia was epic. We needed to investigate. So, we came over several thousand years ago when conflict began and we were called by your ancients. They called for help and assistance. We responded and have been around ever since. We are here to guide you, show you how to work with energy or what some of you would term magic. We have helped those who have asked and promoted their clairvoyance and seeing. We have given instruction to these ancients and slowly these skills have been handed down through the generations of you humans.

Some of you were tortured and killed as others felt threatened. These are the lesser evolved of humans; the power hungry, egotistical humans.

We live both on the inside of the planet and the outside. We meditate in pyramids with specific crystals to enable the world to heal with the energy from us and the crystals. There are times of celebrations and harvests. The majority of the time is spent learning and honing our skills to aid the universes. We teach our offspring just like you teach yours.

We have no conflict, we have no war, we have learned to trust the big picture, our leaders are totally transparent and we all can have a say, we live in total peace and know how rewarding it is to be this way and we want the best for you.

We are here to help… Arnoah.

33.

Feelings
by Quan Yin
(extra)

We want to talk to you of feelings. These are genuine emotions that come from the heart, master and the soul, teacher. What is happening is that the soul - teacher, wants to teach you how to manage these feelings and how to learn by them.

Humans learn more from extremes of emotion and feelings. They are more memorable, either good or bad if they are extreme. Feelings allow you to grow and accumulate sensations and experiences and to start cataloguing them for future experiences and learning.

Emotions come from the head, the ego. Other learned people have written about the ego in this new movement to be more aware and be more mindful. Feelings can change the brain and its patterning. Humans like tradition and schedules, organising and boundaries. This helps the mind to compartmentalise thoughts and feelings. We like patterns for you as it helps to give you structure to cope with daily life, some would say the daily grind but the regularity keeps you safe. Very few can cope with change suddenly and a new direction of the life path. Some cannot cope and it will send them into a spin. It will rock and wobble their world. When they think they have got it all sorted another glitch in their day appears and some cannot cope and may have a breakdown. Others will embrace it and wonder what all the fuss is about. These latter people as we said are few and far between. These are the more adventurous amongst you. These are the ones that can go through life by the seat of their pants and it always turn out well eventually. However, there is often a rocky road to get to that comfortable place again.

The world needs stable people. The way the world and governments are formed the stability of the people is paramount. The governments are for your protection in the world. The jobs that people do help the government run the country. The world cannot have constant travelling otherwise the countries would be unstable and never knowing who will turn up in the work force the following day. What this shows is that you are all different. Instead you must keep learning from your perspective about your feelings and how to navigate through this world and on to the next life.

Feelings are complicated and are of the human design. When you are challenged or hurt this shows in your auric field. The colours get duller and the vibration becomes muted. Ask us and we will support you in your healing process, ask for a passed loved one and they will come. Love hurts and there is no denying that, however, it is a wonderful experience to be able to truly sample and feel the true depths of true love. The first hit of oxytocin is exciting. This is a chemical that humans produce for love, (in your heart and in your brain) as well as for your children's love. This amazing feeling gives you the sensation of your heart bursting with joy and love. However, this cannot be sustained for the long haul. The more solid partnership bases itself on love, companionship, a feeling of belonging, a feeling of completeness, a feeling of security, and above all a great friendship where truths are spoken without hesitation, where acceptance and non-judgement is complete. To be friends first and last is the makings of a sustainable relationship. To know each other first without the game of dating (and many do treat it like a game) lays good foundations and roots. Where visibility is everywhere, no secrets, with complete trust. This serves as a solid base on which to work from and build. If there are differences, then you can discuss and work them out between you. Compromise is a skill and negotiation of what is really important to both of you should be discussed. Look at all the angles and facets of the topic and work out what is best for the both of you and for the relationship. If you have built good foundations, then offence will be at a minimum when openly talking about subjects that are important to you.

Feelings are deep and emotions are shallow. Feelings will give you greater learning and growth. Emotions are about the here and now. The instant hurt, the instant laughter. All can be extreme and feel intense. The way to discern these are by going into yourself and notice where the emotion/feeling is coming from. Centre yourself and feel through your body. Where is this coming from? If it is a feeling you will notice it in your heart or your soul.

When you split from a romantic relationship then you often feel it in your heart, as though your heart is breaking in two. Hence the phrase "the heart is broken" and that is what it feels like. If you weren't so invested in the partnership and it breaks you will probably feel a little disgruntled especially if you weren't the one to call it off. This is the bruised ego because you didn't get in first; the other did. This is different. Often if it is an emotional breakup with the ego and then after a few days you will get used to not texting, communicating and filling in time together and then you can move on. However, if it is feelings in the body that you are experiencing then a process needs to be completed in order to move on with your life. Ways to do this include writing to them about all the good times and the bad times, you can be heartless in your comebacks, a bitch and bring out all of your hurt and negative emotions. Read the words out loud to yourself and burn the papers. This often gives a sense of lightness of the situation after letting the physical letter go. Cry, wail, sob, complain, be down in your own self-pity. This needs to be experienced. All of these intense feelings and emotions need to be felt, sat in and then moved on for the greater good. This is a massive part of personal growth. By experiencing these extremes so the soul can move on and learn. Put healing crystals around your body when sleeping, talk to a friend but don't pester them repeatedly. You have to learn, your soul has to learn. It may be worth doing the write, read burn exercise a few times as the feelings go deep and it is best to process them rather than walking around like a sad sack and expect people to keep being nice and listening. If you keep repeating the same story in the same way then perhaps you need to get special help as this is a sign of trauma. Write, write, write and then read and burn. This is a cleansing process for your soul. When reading it out loud it brings the attentions of angels and loved ones to help you through this. They will be there for you but again you must ask. It is a tried and tested process, so rest assured that this will help heal the pain and process it quickly. However, do not just rush through this process as it is paramount that you feel it and do not deny it. It will make you sick either now or later. The phrase "he died of a broken heart" is not uncommon. Those of you who have unrequited love have it hard. Clearly if the other is not reciprocating then you have got it wrong, or you needed to experience rejection. This is also a lesson in your resilience for you to grow.

In the beginning of dating emotions are running rampant, especially in teenagers and those in their 20s as their hormones are carousing around the body. This has a bearing on how you feel and often make it really intense. They give false readings and once the hormones (oxytocin, serotonin) have settled down as the honeymoon period is coming to an end then it is time to reassess. Is it feelings that you have for this person or is it shallow emotion? If the latter is the case you will often get grumpy with them, or feel disgruntled if you don't get your way. Or the silly little quirks and habits start to irritate you then get out of the relationship. It is not fair on the other person if you are not up front in the relationship. It is better to truly discuss what you feel with each other. This takes guts and strength from within. Fear of your truth will come onto it. For reasons of rejection, (nobody likes rejection as the ego is bruised) fear of being too keen, of frightening them away. All this needs to be discussed instead of a half-truth relationship. Again, it takes practice and this is what you do in the first half of your lives. By the time you get a little older and surer of yourself then it becomes easier. Truth saying is a skill and the delivery is also important. However, don't be too wishy washy as they may not get your point. Be who you have grown into. Be your true self, your authentic self.

Relationships are one of the most challenging dynamics. You spend most of your time with them. If you can be friends first this is often a gentle way of speaking your truth about who you are and your quirks. It gives the other a chance to really know you and you them. You'll know if it is meant to be. If you are really smitten and the other doesn't even notice then it will be worth speaking your truth and see how it goes. There may be rejection but at least you will know where you stand. Then you can either get on with your future lessons or begin an amazing relationship.

Feelings are cultivated, emotions are instant.

That's all for now. Go in love.

Seeing, Feeling, Hearing and Being with Spirit.
A tool to help Gaia and mankind get the best out of your world.

Reincarnation
A process by which your soul comes back to learn the next lessons. The soul can learn and acknowledge the other elements of being a human in order to help others when the soul returns to Source. To experience all forms of the human psyche and personalities so that you learn that the ego does not control the mind but instead the teacher and the master learns to communicate with the human in order to better themselves and the human race. Leading to love, trust, and acceptance with no judgement.

Contract
This is what is agreed before you come to Gaia and it contains the lessons that have been decided upon by you and us. Masters, teachers and loved ones all have a discussion with you to help you learn lessons in the next life. The contract of the next life will contain both good and bad life events depending on what you have agreed to in the life that you are about to be reborn into.

Soul families
These are a group of souls that have been together several times or more to experience life and relationships with these others. They often consist of the same souls just in different bodies. Different dynamics in the families so that you may experience all the different ways a relationship can happen. You will experience either being sister, brother, parent, cousin and even friends.

Twin Flames
This originally started as one soul at Source that worked to enable many to sort out problems and experiences for others. So, this soul grows so big with the vibration of love to help those on earth that it splits into two. The two souls or two halves become a human to help those on this earth with acts of kindness and compassion. To help demonstrate and teach people in their way of love, acceptance and kindness. They can meet if it

is written into their contract. However, they may not be ready for each other. There may be a large difference in age in a life so this will not be the best time to join forces. There is often a chaser and a runner. This refers to the knowledge and lessons that one of them has learnt and the other is slowly getting up to speed. They are two very similar souls as they are from the same at Source. They come together when the time is right to help humanity and begin great work to help Gaia and the souls that need guidance and compassion. They can be in a relationship of romance once all the lessons have been worked through. Together they can combine their power and do great things. If they haven't found each other they will do great work but not to the greatness of the combination of the two souls. That is why we try to bring them together to help humanity. The relationship can be challenging but as they are old souls, they have more understanding and acceptance of the world and of each other. During this relationship they will also learn lessons of themselves and each other.

Teachers

We are the ones who advise and discuss with the masters on how it is best to go forward. We are made up of ascended masters and others from other planets and universes. We help not only mankind but also your masters and loved ones. We guide the loved ones and train them to become helpful guides or angels. We are here for all of you in spirit and humanness. We understand this and many other universes and worlds. We guide you to sustain life and love. We can message you through your subconscious level, we can put visions, pictures and words in to your head to give the messages that you need at that point, either through clairvoyance, mediumship or through these records. We understand more than you think and feel. We are aware of the greater picture, for the greater good, on this planet as in others. We communicate with your soul. Your soul is your teacher and we are in direct communication with your soul. We are all part of the one energy source there are no soul individuals, on a level we are all connected. With telepathy we can connect with you. Some of you have the capacity to receive, for those of you who are working through to your last lives and those who are on their last the signals and messages will become clearer for you. However, if you have been drawn to this book and processes of learning then you are able to speed up this process with practice, stillness and minimising the ego.

Listen, ask, and receive and you will feel the change subtly and gradually more and more you will learn to trust our process with you. You are not alone, it isn't scary although at first it may seem to be. But rest assured this is only temporary.

Gaia

This refers to Mother Earth and the energies that surround the planet. Gaia is of energy and life to help sustain humans in order to learn compromise and love for her. Gaia can pick up on good and bad energies. If they are significant emotional events then Gaia will have an imprint of that energy at that place of happening. It could be good, bad or traumatic. The stronger the energy the more the imprint on Gaia and her energetic network. Gaia, — Mother Earth is very resilient and can sustain a lot of abuse. She can adapt and change depending on the weather conditions and manmade objects. These include buildings and structures that have needed her resources to make.

Source

This is referred to as Heaven in many religions. There is no heaven and hell. There is only Source. This is where heavenly bodies, angels, loved ones (passed friends and family), masters, interplanetary beings and teachers are. This is also where your soul discusses what is to be learnt in the next life, the lessons that will help you grow and learn.

Masters

These are humans who have learnt lessons in their lives past and present. They are grand masters that become revered by the people as they have much wisdom and compassion and very little ego. They have worked through their lives and are now at Source to help humans work through their lives this time. They can choose to repeat a life or stay at Source and help. There is no hierarchy as we are all equal and all you have to do is ask for these masters' help and they will assist. These masters include

Pavarti, Ganesh, Apollo, Kuan Yin, Horus, Serapis bay, Jesus, St, Francis, Mother Mary.

Spirituality
Spirituality is many things to many people. Definitions are different depending on your religious belief. Spirituality from Source is an energetic feeling. It is a knowing that you are not alone in your world it is comfort and love to you and to everything. It is a belief that everything is equal and all on Gaia has a resonance or vibration that communicates with Source. In essence it is love for all.

Channelling
This is where a person is able to take messages from Source and give them to others. Channelling can come in different forms. Through some that just give you messages, through a medium — cards, objects, or just a connection. Or it can be a complete change in person. The host steps back and allows the soul of another to come through to talk to you directly. The host soul is unaware of anything that a spirit says to the receiving party.

Loved Ones
These are your own soul family's guides. They are passed loved ones that can be around you if you call on them. Sometimes they don't want to leave their own loved one still on this earth. They will watch over them until they are more able to cope and heal. Ask them to be with you, and for proof often they will play with electricity. Flicker of lights, television or computer starts behaving unusually.

Ascended Masters
Buddha, Mother Mary, Archangel Michael, Archangel Raphael, Archangel Gabriel, Archangel Uriel, Krishna, Mohammed, Merlin, Guinevere, Oshun, Jesus, Mary Magdalene, Meave, Horus, Yogananda, and many more. Look them up and find out about them. Then you know which is the best Ascended Master to help you with your situation.

Thank you

	Cups (Emotions – Water)	Wands (Will - Fire)	Pentacles (Physical - Earth)	Swords (Power/Intellect - Air)
Ace	Love, Compassion, new creative project	Inspiration, new opportunities, aggression, birth	Attainment, abundance, perfection	Breakthroughs, mental clarity, success takes root
	Clouded joy, loss of faith	False start, distractions, delays, impotency	Corruption, greed, lost opportunity	Clouded judgement, violence, embarrassment
Two	Unified love, partnership, new ideas shared	Future planning, discovery, dominant personality	Multiple priorities, fluctuation of fortune.	Difficult decision, affection, resolution
	Break-ups, disharmony, infidelity	Lack of planning, fear of unknown, pride, desire	Over committed, disorganised, simulated gaiety	Confusion, stalemet, duplicity
Three	Fortunate conclusion, healing, solace	Progress, expansion, possible partnership	Teamwork, collaboration, skilled	Heartbreak, emotion pain, conflict
	Over-indulgence, 3rd party	Questionable, arrogance, lack of foresight	Disharmony, working alone, money problems	Releasing pain, optimism, forgiveness, disorder
Four	Boredom, need to re-evaluate	Celebration, possible romance, prosperity	Saving money, security, conservatism	Rest, relaxation, recuperation, solitude
	knowledge acquired, new possibilities	Inner-harmony, conflict, transition, completion delayed but forthcoming	Over spending, greed, delay	Exhaustion, burn-out, stagnation, economy
Five	Regret, failure, disappointment	Conflict, disagreement, tension, obstacles	Financial loss, lack, worry, material loss	Conflict, disagreement, winning at all cost, defeat
	Self-forgiveness, moving on, reunion	Conflict avoidance, trickery	Recovery from financial loss, disharmony in love	Reconciliation, inner strength required, indecision
Six	Harmony, joy from hardwork, success	Success, victory, advancement	Giving, receiving, generosity, charity	Transition, putting swords down, releasing of baggage
	Living in the past blocks present success	Fall from grace, delayed rewards, red tape	Unpaid debts, one-sided charity, envy, theft	Stalemate, unfinished business, struggle
Seven	Thought to opportunities, illusions	Challenge, success, victory, protection	Long term view, investment, growth	Change or job/residence,confidence
	Alignment, values, determination	Exhaustion, overwhelmed, timidity due to unknown fear	Lack of LT view, imprudent actions	Imposter, keeping secret, reluctance to finish
Eight	Disappointment, abandonment, turning point	Rapid movement, news	Apprenticeship, mastery, development, savings	Negative thoughts, imprisonment, victim
	Reckless, restless, pleasure seeking	Delays, frustration, resisting change	Perfectionism, hypocrisy, dishonest	Releasing self-limiting beliefs, open, freedom
Nine	Contentment, wishes fulfilled, abundance, opposition	Resilience, test of faith, boundaries, victory against opposition	Abundance, luxury, surprise money	Anxiety, worry, fear, nightmares
	Dissatisfaction, indulgence, material losses	Struggle, defensive, paranoia, over coming barriers	Over-investment, hustling, time to analyse goals	Deep-seated fears, secrets, need to trust in Divine for solace
Ten	Divine love, honor, security	Burden, responsibility, problems near resolutions	Wealth, financial security, LT success	Painful endings, betrayal, loss, crisis
	Disconnection, stagnation, unhappiness	Carrying the burden, misuse of talents	Dark side of wealth, financial loss, litigation	Recovery, regeneration, resisting and inevitable end
Page/ Prince	Creative opportunities, reflective, loyal	Inspiration, limitless potential, trustworthy	Manifestation, financial opportunity, conscientious	New ideas, curiosity, thirst for knowledge, grace
	Creative blocks, immaturity, deception	Redirecting energy, limiting beliefs, instability	Procrastination, lack of progress, wasteful	All talk no action, haphazard, haste, powerless
Knight/ Princess	Romance, charm	Energy, passion, inspired action, journey, sudden life changes	Hard work, productivity, conservatism	Ambitious, action-orientated, fast, heroism
	Overactive, jealous	Haste, frustration, delays, breakup	Boredom, feeling stuck, perfectionism,narrow minded	Restless, unfocused, impulsive, secretive
Queen	Compassionate, stable, psychic ability	Confidence, determination, social, practical	Nurturing, practical, charity, shrewd, noble soul	Independent, unbiased, boundaries, awareness of suffering, perceptice
	Dishonest, perverse,self love	Introverted, obstinate, possessive	Distrustful, insecure, suspicious	Overly emotional, cold hearted, vengeful
King	Emotionally balanced, diplomatic, kind	Natural born leader, vision, honour, devoted	Wealth, business, leadership, abundance	Mental clarity, intellectual power, truth
	Moodiness, manipulative, injustice	Impulsiveness, haste, ruthless, opposing	Inept, obsessed with wealth and status,	Quiet power, misuse, manipulation

0 – The Fool	**Upright:** New beginnings, innocence, a free spirit, choose wisely. **Reversed:** Holding back, recklessness, risk-taker, re-evaluate
1 – The Magician	**Upright:** Manifestation, resourcefulness, inspired action, integrity. **Reversed:** Manipulation, poor planning, selfish ends.
2 – The High Priestess	**Upright:** Intuition, sacred knowledge, divine feminine, busy times. **Reversed:** Secrets, , withdrawn, let go of old patterns.
3 – The Empress	**Upright:** Femininity, beauty, nurturing, abundance. **Reversed:** Creative block, dependence on others, depression.
4 – The Emperor	**Upright:** Authority, establishment, father figure. **Reversed:** Domination, excess control, inflexibility, undisciplined.
5 – The Hierophant	**Upright:** Spiritual wisdom, religious beliefs, tradition. **Reversed:** Freedom, challenging the status quo, explore new horizons.
6 – The Lovers	**Upright:** Love, relationships, harmony, balance energies. **Reversed:** Disharmony, imbalance, misalignment. Centre within.
7 – The Chariot	**Upright:** Willpower, determination, solid movement, victory. **Reversed:** Opposition, lack of direction, overwhelmed circumstances.
8 – Strength	**Upright:** Strength, courage, compassion. **Reversed:** Self-doubt, low energy, raw emotion, abuse of power. Centre within
9 – The Hermit	**Upright:** Soul-searching, being alone, inner guidance. **Reversed:** Isolation, loneliness, withdrawal. Let go, let God/dess come through
10 – The Wheel of Fortune	**Upright:** Good luck, life cycles, destiny. **Reversed:** Bad luck, resistance to change, breaking cycles. Keep faith, it will pass
11 – Justice	**Upright:** Fairness, truth, cause and effect. **Reversed:** Unfairness, lack of accountability, dishonesty. Don't be a victim.
12 – The Hanged Man/Transition	**Upright:** Release, surrender, awaiting new perspectives. **Reversed:** Delays, resistance, stalling. Time to let go
13 – Death	**Upright:** Endings, change, transformation, have faith. **Reversed:** Resistance to change. Need for new ideas to motivate.
14 – Temperance	**Upright:** Balance, moderation, patience. **Reversed:** Imbalance, excess, realignment. Time to reassess activities.
15 – The Devil/The Deceiver	**Upright:** Shadow self, attachment, restriction. **Reversed:** Release from restrictions, gain spiritual understanding and freedom
16 – The Tower	**Upright:** Sudden change, upheaval, awakening. **Reversed:** Entrapment, feeling imprisoned. This too will pass
17 – The Star	**Upright:** Hopes and dreams, faith, spirituality. **Reversed:** Lack of faith, despair, disconnection. Be true and rise above adversity
18 – The Moon	**Upright:** Intuition, sub-conscience, illusion. Percieve the truth **Reversed:** Deception, repressed emotion, inner confusion.
19 – The Sun	**Upright:** Positivity, success, vitality, yes! **Reversed:** Poverty of spirit, feeling down. Trust the sun will shine.
20 – Judgement	**Upright:** Rebirth, inner calling, absolution. **Reversed:** Self-doubt, ignoring the intuition, assess the facts, choose to be free.
21 – The World/ The Universe	**Upright:** Completion, integration, accomplishment, travel. **Reversed:** Imperfection, fear impedes. Avail yourself to new ideas.

The above tables were put together over a meta analysis of many tarot decks and have been summarised for easy access to explanations. However, it is all your own interpretation. These are the basic meanings. They can all change slightly depending on the position and who you are doing a reading for. The upper meaning (blue) is for the upright card, and the lower meaning (white) is for the card reversed. Feel the card, hold it in your hand and allow the messages to come through. Have fun.